The Thirteen Colonies

Maryland

Books in the Thirteen Colonies series include:

The Thirteen Colonies

Maryland

Tom Streissguth

Lucent Books, Inc.
P.O. Box 289011, San Diego, California

Library of Congress Cataloging-in-Publication Data

Streissguth, Thomas, 1958–
  Maryland / by Thomas Streissguth.
    p. cm. — (The thirteen colonies)
Includes bibliographical references (p.) and index.
  ISBN 1-56006-871-X (hardback : alk. paper)
  1. Maryland—History—Colonial period, ca. 1600–1775—Juvenile
literature. 2. Maryland—History—Revolution, 1775–1783—Juvenile
literature. 3. Maryland—History—War of 1812—Juvenile literature.
[1. Maryland—History—Colonial period, ca. 1600–1775.] I. Title.
II. Thirteen colonies (Lucent Books)
  F184 .S94 2002
  975.2'02—dc21

                                                    2001001339

Contents

Foreword

T he story of the thirteen English colonies that became the United States of America is one of startling diversity, conflict, and cultural evolution. Today, it is easy to assume that the colonists were of one mind when fighting for independence from England and afterwards when the national government was created. However, the American colonies had to overcome a vast reservoir of distrust rooted in the broad geographical, economic, and social differences that separated them. Even the size of the colonies contributed to the conflict; the smaller states feared domination by the larger ones.

These sectional differences stemmed from the colonies' earliest days. The northern colonies were more populous and their economies were more diverse, being based on both agriculture and manufacturing. The southern colonies, however, were dependent on agriculture—in most cases, the export of only one or two staple crops. These economic differences led to disagreements over things such as the trade embargo the Continental Congress imposed against England during the war. The southern colonies wanted their staple crops to be exempt from the embargo because their economies would have collapsed if they could not trade with England, which in some cases was the sole importer. A compromise was eventually made and the southern colonies were allowed to keep trading some exports.

In addition to clashing over economic issues, often the colonies did not see eye-to-eye on basic political philosophy. For example, Connecticut leaders held that education was the route to greater political liberty, believing that knowledgeable citizens would not allow themselves to be stripped of basic freedoms and rights. South Carolinians, on the other hand, thought that the protection of personal property and economic independence was the basic foundation of freedom. In light of such profound differences it is amazing that the colonies were able to unite in the fight for independence and then later under a strong national government.

Why, then, did the colonies unite? When the Revolutionary War began the colonies set aside their differences and banded together because they shared a common goal—gaining political freedom from what they considered a tyrannical monarchy—that could be more easily attained if they cooperated with each other. However, after the war ended, the states abandoned unity and once again pursued sectional interests, functioning as little nations in a weak confederacy. The congress of this confederacy, which was bound by the Articles of Confederation, had virtually no authority over the individual states. Much bickering ensued— the individual states refused to pay their war debts to the national government, the nation was sinking further into an economic depression, and there was nothing the national government could do. Political leaders realized that the nation was in jeopardy of falling apart. They were also aware that European nations such as England, France, and Spain were all watching the new country, ready to conquer it at the first opportunity. Thus the states came together at the Constitutional Convention in order to create a system of government that would be both strong enough to protect them from invasion and yet nonthreatening to state interests and individual liberties.

The Thirteen Colonies series affords the reader a thorough understanding of how the development of the individual colonies helped create the United States. The series examines the early history of each colony's geographical region, the founding and first years of each colony, daily life in the colonies, and each colony's role in the American Revolution. Emphasis is given to the political, economic, and social uniqueness of each colony. Both primary and secondary quotes enliven the text, and sidebars highlight personalities, legends, and personal stories. Each volume ends with a chapter on how the colony dealt with changes after the war and its role in developing the U.S. Constitution and the new nation. Together, the books in this series convey a remarkable story—how thirteen fiercely independent colonies came together in an unprecedented political experiment that not only succeeded, but endures to this day.

Introduction

A Practical Utopia

In 1524 Italian navigator Giovanni da Verrazano arrived off the coast of North America, sailed north from the Outer Banks, a narrow strip of barrier islands in present-day North Carolina, and then passed the wide inlet to a long, northward-stretching saltwater bay. Several rivers emptied into this bay, their waters rising and falling with the tides of the sea. To da Verrazano's sailors, this dark green land held strange wonders and terrifying dangers. Opportunity lay here as well, for those willing to move ashore, build new homes, and risk hunger and death in a distant and lonely country.

Italian navigator Giovanni da Verrazano explored Maryland's Chesapeake Bay in 1524.

A century later the king of England granted a charter to Cecilius Calvert, Lord Baltimore. The charter made the land adjoining Chesapeake Bay, and north of the Potomac River, Calvert's personal property. As "proprietor" of Maryland, Calvert would be free to settle and develop this wilderness as he saw fit. He would make the rules, choose the governors, and collect the rents from English colonists who would journey across the Atlantic Ocean to Maryland.

Calvert wanted to avoid the mistakes of earlier colonists—especially those in Massachusetts and Virginia—who had fought with Native Americans, struggled to cultivate poor soil in rough climates, and experienced religious conflict within their own communities. He wanted to run Maryland as a practical business, one that should be spared the troubles of those who had already arrived in North America.

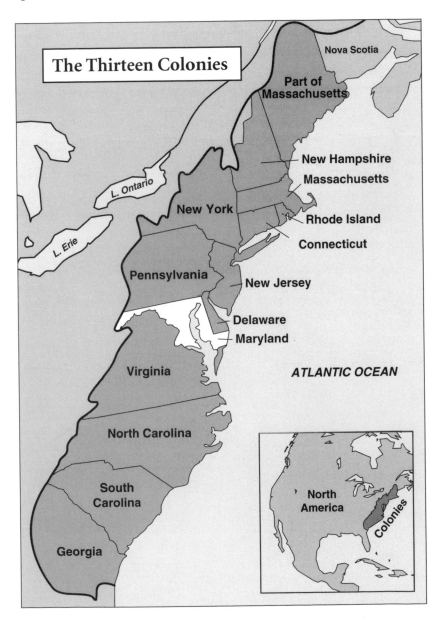

The Thirteen Colonies

He asked his brother, Leonard, to sail to Maryland with the first colonists. Instead of defeating the Indians, Leonard was to make peace with them. Instead of establishing an official church, he was to foster religious tolerance. And instead of practicing subsistence agriculture, Marylanders would grow a profitable cash crop, tobacco, which could be sold and traded for the goods they needed.

For these reasons, colonial Maryland represented a kind of practical utopian experiment in the wilderness. But for all of Calvert's careful preparation, the colony did not escape disputes, dissension, or Indian trouble. Maryland's history was as turbulent as any other colony's, and after 150 years of proprietors, most Marylanders demanded the end of the Calverts' rule and the independence of the United States.

Chapter One

The English Arrive in Chesapeake Bay

T he charter of the Maryland colony, granted to Cecilius Calvert, Lord Baltimore, made the territory into the personal fiefdom of a single family. This had important consequences for Maryland's colonial history. Before the first European settlers could arrive, Calvert's claim to the land was disputed by a clan of English traders who had already reached the Chesapeake. Maryland would also see a clash of interests between the aristocratic, town-dwelling Calverts and the rural settlers who lived and worked in the new land. Conflicts over land and over political authority would make the colony a contentious place throughout the seventeenth century.

The Susquehannock

The land that would become Maryland was inhabited long before the Calverts laid claim to it. People had been living along Chesapeake Bay and its tributaries for more than ten thousand years. Europeans arriving to settle Maryland found many reminders of the colony's previous inhabitants: grooved axes, soapstone bowls, fragments of pottery, and arrowheads. At some points along the shore, mounds of clams and oyster shells lay where these early Americans had dumped the remains of their ancient meals.

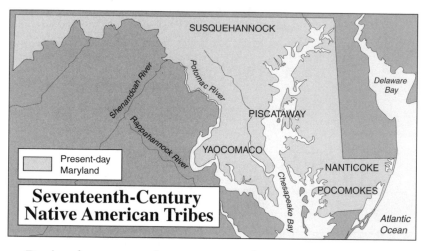

Seventeenth-Century Native American Tribes

During the seventeenth century, several peaceful Indian tribes were living along Chesapeake Bay. On the eastern shore were Algonquian-speaking Nanticokes and Pocomokes. On the western shore lived the Piscataway. The largest and strongest tribe in the region, the Susquehannock, belonged to the nation of the Iroquois.

Like the English settlers and the Algonquian tribes, the Susquehannock favored the riverbanks as sites to build their homes and plant their crops. For protection, they surrounded their villages with palisades of tall wooden staves, cut from the sturdiest trees in the surrounding forests. Within the walls, the Susquehannock raised huts of saplings covered with bark.

Susquehannock women grew squash, corn, potatoes, beans, and peas. They stored their crops in clay-lined pits dug into the earth. When food was scarce they gathered nuts, such as acorns and walnuts, as well as berries. Using log canoes, the men cast nets and lines to catch the abundant fish in the bay and its tributaries. The salty tidewater—the bays and river estuaries that rose and fell with the ocean tides—also sheltered clams, crabs, mussels, and oysters. The forests provided good hunting for deer, black bear, fox, otter, turkey, and beaver.

It was in the early 1600s that the Indians of the Chesapeake first saw tall ships sailing along their shores. One of these ships was commanded by the English captain John Smith. In 1608 Captain Smith set out from Jamestown, farther south in the colony of Virginia. Smith carefully maneuvered his ship among the muddy shoals and meandering shores, searching out promising land with a long spyglass. In several places he met friendly Indians who offered his crew gifts of arrows, pipes, and small fur pelts. In his writings Smith also recalled less friendly encounters:

> The people ran as amazed in groups from place to place, and ... they were not sparing of their arrowes, nor the greatest passion they could express of their anger. . . . The next day they came unarmed, with every one a basket, dancing in a ring, to draw us on shore: but seeing there was nothing in them but villainy, we discharged a volly of muskets charged with pistoll shot, whereat they all lay tumbling on the grownd. [1]

Smith and other English captains believed that the Indians could be overcome and the land made productive. One crucial ingredient was required: settlers. A large group of English families must be willing to give up their homes, brave a long sea voyage, and work like slaves. They would have to endure harsh weather and, at some point, defend themselves against the Native Americans.

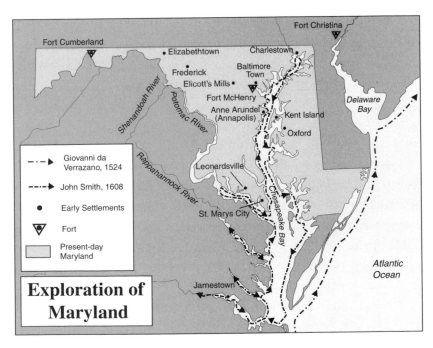

John Smith Discovers a Stingray

Captain John Smith's voyage into the Chesapeake Bay presented him and his crew with dangers both human and animal. One account of a companion, described in Hubert Footner's Rivers of the Eastern Shore, *describes Smith's encounter with one of the bay's more hazardous fishes.*

"But it chanced our Captain taking a fish from his sword (not knowing her condition) being much of the fashion of a Thornbacke but having a long tayle [tail] like a riding rodde, whereon the middest is a most poisoned sting of two or three inches long, bearded like a saw on each side, which she strucke into the wrist of his arme near an inch and a halfe; no bloud [blood] nor wound was seene, but a little blew spot, but the torment was instantly so extreme, that in foure hours had so swollen his hand, arme and shoulder, we all with much sorrow concluded his funerall, and prepared his grave in an island hard by, as himselfe directed, yet it pleased God by a previously oyle [oil] Dr. Russell at the first applyed to it with a probe, ere night his tormenting paine was so well asswaged [assuaged] that he ate of the fish to his supper."

George Calvert's Charter

The settlement of North America had already begun under the watchful eyes of the king of England, who claimed all of this land by right of its discovery by English sea captains such as Smith. On the other side of the Atlantic, there was already a fierce competition for the king's royal charters—the documents that granted North America's new colonies to the lucky and ambitious few.

George Calvert was one such ambitious Englishman, believing that North America held great riches in the form of cultivable land, minerals, and timber. Calvert had shown loyalty to King James I, and in 1621 the king rewarded him with a colony in Newfoundland, a rocky coast lying far to the north of Chesapeake Bay. But the Newfoundland settlement could not cope with the poor growing conditions and harsh weather, and it quickly failed.

Calvert did not give up. After abandoning Newfoundland, he moved south, to a warmer place: Virginia. The warmer climate and better soil of Virginia promised productive crops of corn, wheat, and tobacco. But the colony had already been chartered to a group of investors, and the people in Virginia did not take kindly to George Calvert. In their eyes, he belonged to the wrong church—he had converted to the Roman Catholic rites.

A Last Try

Catholics had long been a minority in England, where the crown had established the Anglican Church as the official state religion. Seventeenth-century England had become a three-way religious battleground between Catholics, Anglicans, and "Dissenters," who belonged to smaller Protestant sects such as the Puritans and the Quakers. Finding persecution at the hands of the Anglican Church and the English government, these Dissenters were now making their way to the shores of North America. In Massachusetts, Virginia, and (much later) Pennsylvania, their leaders could practice their faith and follow their doctrines in peace.

In Virginia, that meant trouble for Calvert, as historian Matthew Page Andrews relates:

It was sufficient for many of the Virginians to know that Lord Baltimore [the title bestowed on Calvert] was . . . a Roman Catholic peer. . . . These transplanted Englishmen had been threatened, from the date of their first settlement, with extinction by the power of Spain, whose New World claims had been formally sanctioned by the [Roman Catholic] pope; hence, many of them made no distinction between an English adherent of the Church of Rome and an out-and-out enemy. [2]

In 1632 Englishman George Calvert became the first Lord Baltimore.

Calvert left Virginia, returned to England, and in 1632 was rewarded with another colonial charter. The new charter allowed Calvert to settle land extending north from the Potomac River, from the Alleghenies to the Delaware River.

Before the king could affix his royal seal to the charter of Maryland, Lord Baltimore died. The charter then passed to his son Cecilius, the second Lord Baltimore. At the king's request, Cecilius Calvert named the colony Maryland, after Charles's queen, Henrietta Maria.

By this charter, Lord Baltimore and his heirs could claim the title *proprietor*—a man who had the right to settle and govern the colony as he saw fit. In *Tidewater Maryland*, author Paul Wilstach explains: "The proprietor exercised semi-regal prerogatives. He virtually was king in his tidewater domain. His office was hereditary, and he was privileged to create courts and appoint the judges of them, to pardon criminals, and to grant titles."[3]

The Calverts of Maryland would also have the right to appoint governors and all other colonial officials as well as the right to appoint a council. The proprietor alone had the right to write laws that applied to the Maryland settlers (although he was also supposed to have the colonists' assent to these laws). He would decide who would be granted land to settle and farm, and he would have the right to collect "quitrents" paid by English settlers for the use of the land. Calvert expected to profit through the collection of quitrents and by taking a

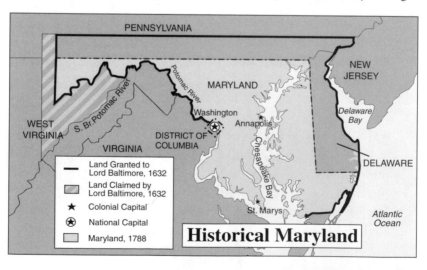

Historical Maryland

PENNSYLVANIA
NEW JERSEY
MARYLAND
Potomac River
Washington
Annapolis
Delaware Bay
WEST VIRGINIA
S. Br. Potomac River
VIRGINIA
DISTRICT OF COLUMBIA
Chesapeake Bay
DELAWARE
St. Marys
Atlantic Ocean

Land Granted to Lord Baltimore, 1632
Land Claimed by Lord Baltimore, 1632
★ Colonial Capital
⊛ National Capital
Maryland, 1788

share of the duties charged on goods exported from and imported into Maryland. For Cecilius Calvert and his heirs, Maryland was no more, and no less, than a business.

The Colony's Early Days

Calvert gathered the first party of Maryland settlers in the fall of 1633. He called for brave young men and women who were willing to chance the voyage and the many dangers of North America. He placed his brother, Leonard, in charge of the expedition. Two ships, the *Ark* and the *Dove*, were prepared for the passage. On November 22, 1633, they sailed with about 250 settlers aboard.

The winter voyage over the North Atlantic Ocean turned out to be the settlers' worst experience. Strong and cold winds buffeted the ships, forcing the passengers to remain belowdecks. The hatches remained closed; the foul air was sickening to breathe. The cooks on board had only salted meat, bread, and water to set out on the rough plank dining tables. Several passengers grew sick, threatening an epidemic that could have ended their lives as surely as a shipwreck in the open sea.

The passage to North America lasted a long five months. Soon after leaving England, the *Ark* and the *Dove* were separated in a storm. Both sailed south to the warm and calmer waters of the West Indies before they were reunited. In the islands they took on water and supplies. Finally, on March 25, 1634, the *Ark* and the *Dove* reached the wide mouth of the Potomac River, where the river flows into Chesapeake Bay.

From the decks of their ships, the colonists had little to see along the banks of the Potomac. Tall trees, clinging to muddy beaches and small, mossy hillocks, lined the shore. The smoke of a few campfires could be seen rising from the clearings. At the low-lying island known as St. Clements, the house and shop of an English trader stood among the strange bark-covered huts of an Indian village.

At the new village they called St. Marys City, the colonists explored the first dry land their feet had known for months. They had many questions of the trader, a lonely Englishman named Henry Fleet. Their most urgent questions involved these Indian huts. The settlers

Colonists kneel in prayer after landing along the shores of the Chesapeake Bay in 1634.

had come well armed and prepared for a fight—they had heard many tales of the bloodshed between colonists and Native Americans in Virginia as well as New England.

Knowing that Virginia and Massachusetts had already suffered bloody clashes with Native Americans, Cecilius Calvert was determined to keep the Maryland Indians friendly. He instructed his brother to trade with the Indians as much as possible and to make treaties instead of making war. The Calverts may not have yet realized, while preparing for their Maryland venture, that the most serious challenge to their claim would come from English, not Indian, rivals.

At St. Marys City

To the relief of Governor Calvert and his settlers, the group learned that the Indian village on St. Clements Island belonged to the peaceful Yaocomaco, allied to the Algonquian-speaking Piscataway. Leonard Calvert offered the Yaocomacos blankets, knives, axes, and other implements in exchange for a long stretch of land along the St. Marys River.

The Yaocomaco, for their part, were willing to cooperate. They saw these strange white people, with their weapons and goods, as welcome future allies in any trouble they might have with the Susquehannock. According to Andrews, "The Yaocomaco Indians had been suffering so greatly from the raids of the more warlike Susquehanna that they were making preparations to leave their homes. They were, therefore, glad to dispose, at some profit to themselves, of property they were about to abandon; and, at the same time, gain an ally against their foes."[4]

The settlers would supply the Yaocomaco with finished goods the Indians lacked: knives, jewelry, blankets, metal goods, and trinkets. For a time, the Indians would share the land with the English. They would direct the settlers to good fishing and hunting. They would serve as guides and scouts in the unknown forests and in the hills rising away from the valley of the Potomac River.

The settlers were soon at work planting fields of corn for their own kitchens and for trade with the other colonies. Fruit trees brought

Leonard Calvert and his settlers offered the Yaocomaco tribe members gifts in exchange for land along the St. Marys River.

William Claiborne, who operated this trading post on Kent Island years before the Calverts' arrival, challenged their claim to Maryland.

from England could also be planted in the clearings and along the shore. There was plenty of game and fish, and across the Atlantic a proprietor determined to make the Maryland colony succeed. There would be no starvation here—but there would be plenty of trouble, caused by the bitter rivalries between Englishmen over the North American colonies.

The Troublesome Mr. Claiborne

Not all of the king's subjects obeyed the royal charters. In the rush for land, conflicts arose and sometimes led to violence. Three years before the *Ark* and the *Dove* arrived, William Claiborne had built his own trading post on Kent Island in Chesapeake Bay. Claiborne and a group of settlers on Kent Island opposed the Calvert family and the charter granted to Lord Baltimore. They were Protestants, and they considered the Catholic Calverts as rivals. Asserting his own claims to the land north of the Potomac, Claiborne defied Lord Baltimore's rights as the proprietor of Maryland.

For Lord Baltimore's settlers, trouble with Claiborne began immediately. Claiborne spread rumors among the Indians that the new

The Battle of Pocomoke Sound

The conflict between Lord Baltimore's settlers and William Claiborne reached its climax at the mouth of the Pocomoke River, where the two sides fought one of the earliest naval battles in the English colonies. In the fall of 1634, after the Marylanders seized one of Claiborne's ships, the *Long Tayle*, Claiborne stole a ship from the wharf at St. Marys and brought it to Kent Island. To goad Claiborne again, the Marylanders sent traders to the eastern shore, at the mouth of the Pocomoke River, a territory Claiborne often worked himself.

Claiborne prepared for war. He ordered one of his ships, the *Cockatrice*, to engage the Marylanders at Pocomoke Sound. On April 23, 1635, the *Cockatrice* sailed into the shallow waters of the sound. The thirteen crew members watched as two enemy ships, the *St. Helen* and the *St. Margaret*, approached with a silvery row of muskets leveled. Lord Baltimore's ships were larger, heavier, and better armed, yet the *Cockatrice* sailed defiantly nearby, its crew brandishing their own long guns. A volley thundered across the shallow water, followed by a menacing plume of black smoke. The deadly rain of lead shot slammed into the plank sides and the sails of the *Cockatrice*, killing Lieutenant Warren, master of the ship, along with two of his crew.

The battle settled nothing in the ongoing rivalry between Claiborne and Calvert. Lord Baltimore would be fighting many more battles, both on the ground and in the English courts, before his title to Maryland was free from all rival claims.

Claiborne and Lord Baltimore's settlers exchange fire during the deadly Battle of Pocomoke Sound.

arrivals were really Spaniards who would enslave the natives and steal their land. Claiborne and soldiers loyal to him fought several skirmishes with the Maryland settlers, including the deadly Battle of Pocomoke Sound. For two years Claiborne held to the eastern shore, carrying out his business despite the Marylanders. In 1636, when Claiborne returned to England, George Evelin, his English overseer, arrived to take control of Kent Island. But Evelin's interest was peaceful trade, not civil war. With the blessing of Governor Calvert and the Maryland colony, Evelin assumed the title of governor of Kent Island and promised to cooperate with Lord Baltimore's men.

Claiborne did not give up the fight. He would spend many years in England, opposing the Calverts and trying to claim his own rights in Maryland. In the meantime, the colony seized his property. When the Kent Islanders again grew troublesome, the Marylanders invaded Kent Island, burned homes, took prisoners, seized trading goods, and strung up several Kent Islanders on a swiftly built gallows. George Evelin, swearing his loyalty to Governor Calvert, was rewarded Kent Island as his private estate.

The Head-Right System

As practical businessmen, the Calverts knew there was more to the success of a colony than peace with the Indians and with the Claibornes. The colony was meant above all to turn a profit, and the Calverts ran their business as any such risky venture must be run: with absolute authority over trade and over land rights. The Marylanders served as their tenants and employees, and they would have to follow the laws and the plan set down by the proprietors.

To settle Maryland with newcomers from England, the Calverts worked according to a practical scheme known as the head-right system. This system was meant to bring as many heads (people) as possible into the colony in the shortest amount of time. Each immigrant had the right to one hundred acres of land. (Artisans such as masons and carpenters received additional land for building their workshops, yards, warehouses, stables, and any other necessities.) The settlers were entitled to land for each additional person who traveled with them, whether they were family members or servants. In the first year of settlement, Lord Baltimore granted two thousand acres to each

Lord Baltimore's Instructions

Religious conflict was brewing in England, and religious intolerance marked the governance of the Massachusetts colony. In his written instructions to Leonard Calvert, his brother, the second Lord Baltimore began with a plea for unity and peace above all. This excerpt is quoted in Edward C. Papenfuse's "An Act Concerning Religion: April 21, 1649: An Interpretation and Tribute to the Citizen Legislators of Maryland."

"His Lordship requires his said Governor and Commissioners that in their voyage to Mary Land they be very careful to preserve unity and peace among all the passengers on shipboard, and that they suffer no scandal nor offence to be given to any of the Protestants, whereby any just complaint may hereafter be made by them in Virginia or in England, and that for that end, they cause all acts of Roman Catholic religion to be done as privately as may be, and that they instruct all the Roman Catholics to be silent upon all occasions of discourse concerning matters of religion; and that the said Governor and Commissioners treat the Protestants with as much mildness and favor as justice will permit. And this (is) to be observed at land as well as at sea."

settler who brought five or more heads. (After the first year, this grant was reduced to one thousand acres.)

Not all Maryland settlers were entitled to land. Most of them came as indentured servants, who had no right to property of any kind except the clothes on their backs. These servants signed agreements to work for a term of four or five years. In exchange for their labor, they were given room and board and a grant of fifty acres of their own if they survived their term of service. For landowners, indentured servants provided the labor that was vital to taming the wilderness, building homes and stables, and producing cash crops for market.

These landowners also could turn to transported criminals, prisoners of war, and refugees. Many of the prisoners had fought for the losing side during the civil wars in England. Instead of being freed, they were sent to the colonies to avoid any further trouble. Criminals had only execution to look forward to if they remained in England. For these condemned men and women, transportation to North

America meant a reprieve from a death sentence. After serving a term of seven years as servants, they became free citizens of the Maryland colony. One Marylander supported the idea:

> I confess I am one of those who think a young country cannot be settled, cultivated, and improved, without people of some sort, and that it is much better for the country to receive convicts than slaves. . . . The wicked and bad of them that come in this Province, mostly run away to the northward, mix with other people, and pass for honest men; whilst those, more innocent, and who come for very light offenses, serve their time out here, behave well, and become useful people.[5]

Any colonist bringing enough individuals for a grant of two thousand acres also had the right to a manor—an estate on which the owner had the right to settle disputes among any tenants and to act as a semi-independent proprietor. In all, sixty-one manors were established in Maryland during the seventeenth century. The colonial barons who owned these prized manors made up Maryland's colonial aristocracy. In imitation of the aristocrats in their old homeland, these landowners held tight to the reigns of local government. Although they had won their land thanks to the Calverts, many of them saw in the New World an opportunity to establish their own small and independent realms in which they obeyed the law and the authorities—including the Calverts—as they pleased.

The Maryland Assembly

Seventeenth-century Maryland resembled a small feudal kingdom, with the distant Lord Baltimore on the colony's throne as landlord, principal landowner, supreme judge, and lawgiver. As settlers continued to arrive, however, some began to oppose the proprietor's absolute rights. In 1635 the colony convened the first meeting of a popular assembly at St. Marys. All of the colony's free men were required to attend. Those who could not had to send a proxy (substitute).

Lord Baltimore saw the Maryland Assembly as a challenge to his rights. In his opinion, the charter gave him—and not the settlers—the right to set down and enforce the law in Maryland. He promptly vetoed all of the measures passed by the assembly. He sent his own rules and instructions back across the Atlantic. When the assembly met again, in 1638, the members immediately took up the question of Lord Baltimore's laws, as described by historian Aubrey C. Land:

Many Maryland colonists opposed the absolute rule of Cecil Calvert.

> On the second day "was read out the draught of the Lawes transmitted by the Lord Proprietor . . . And were severally debated by the house." Next day on the question, "whether they should be received as Lawes or no," the Assembly voted two to one against the proprietor. Then after their flat veto of the Lord Proprietor's proposed laws, the Assembly appointed a committee to draw up its own slate of acts to be debated and forwarded to Lord Baltimore.[6]

The battle of vetoes and competing laws continued until August 21 of that year, when, for the sake of peace, Lord Baltimore agreed that the assembly could write its own laws and that his appointed governor would give his consent to them.

This would not be the last dispute between the Maryland Assembly and the proprietors. Although the proprietors wanted to write their own laws and rules for Maryland, the members of the assembly favored the English common law. This collection of decisions and statutes, recorded over many centuries, applied within the borders of England. If Maryland adopted the common law, then the colonists would have the same rights and responsibilities as any ordinary citizen of the home country.

The proprietor had a very different idea. Lord Baltimore wanted only those English laws that mentioned the colonies to be enforced in

Richard Ingle: Parliament's Privateer

A pirate who saw an opportunity in England's civil war, Richard Ingle won the distinction of being the first sea captain to be granted letters of marque by the English Parliament. These documents authorized Ingle to seize any ship he deemed hostile to Parliament or any ship that traded with those who defied parliamentary authority. By Ingle's reckoning, Parliament's instructions made Catholic Maryland a ripe target for plunder.

After being granted the letters of marque, Ingle, who had already been convicted of piracy in Maryland, returned to the colony for his revenge. After his ship, the *Reformation*, reached St. Marys in February 1645, Ingle seized land, tobacco, and property from Maryland Catholics. He demanded that all Maryland colonists take an oath against Lord Baltimore and the king. Any colonist who refused risked losing his property to Ingle and his well-armed companions. As a result, hundreds of settlers fled Maryland for the safety of Virginia. Ingle then redistributed to Protestants within the colony any property he could not sell and sailed back to England with his loot in April 1645.

Maryland. All other statutes would be subject to his approval. The governor's council, whose members were appointed by the proprietor, supported his position. But as the voice of the free settlers in Maryland, the assembly held power and authority of its own. Its members insisted that they also have a say in how the colony should be governed and run.

Lord Baltimore could not prevent the assembly from meeting without imposing a dictatorship, which would be very bad for business. The assembly was the colony's only representative body in which delegates were elected by the free men of each county. Gradually a balance of power was reached in which the governor's council, which represented the interests of the proprietor, evolved into the assembly's "upper house" (these two bodies—the council and assembly—formed the origins of the two-house legislature that exists in Maryland to this day). But in the meantime, many questions of law and authority needed to be settled, and there would be many years of hostility and conflict between the two camps fighting to and profit from Maryland.

Chapter Two

Religious Strife in Maryland

I n the assembly debates, colonists opposed to proprietary power had banded together to form country party. This faction was made up of men who lived in the country and benefited from the land (unlike the proprietors, who lived in cities in North America and in England). The party claimed rights for the settlers of Maryland and worked against the further enrichment and authority of the proprietors. Underlying this conflict was a fundamental religious quarrel that defied an easy solution.

The Calverts were Catholics, yet a majority of Maryland settlers were Protestants. Lord Baltimore wanted his colony to avoid the religious strife that was tearing at English society and that also affected the North American colonies. Although the Maryland Assembly did pass a religious toleration act, it could not avoid many bitter conflicts over land rights and political power. Much of this conflict had the clash of Protestant and Catholic at its heart. It would not be resolved until Marylanders had to face the much more serious question of independence for all of the English colonies.

The Problem of Quitrents

Many Protestant settlers and landowners suspected the Catholic proprietor of opposing their interests. They also disliked the economic benefits Lord Baltimore drew from the colony. According to a law passed by the assembly, the proprietor was paid one-half of all export duties on tobacco, fourteen pence per ton of cargo brought into the colony, and his "quitrent," paid at the rate of two pence per pound of tobacco grown on any settler's land.

The quitrent was a small tribute paid by the settler to the owner of the land he settled. Some colonists accepted it as a normal cost of living and working on somebody else's land. But for many others, and especially for the Puritans, quitrents were a form of serfdom, a relic of the medieval past. The Puritans believed that any settler who worked and improved the wilderness should be rewarded with clear title to it. This stance threatened the profits made by the proprietors from Maryland, who fought for quitrents and other privileges well into the eighteenth century.

Claiborne Returns

The conflict in the colonies echoed that in the home country, where a political revolution was being carried out by members of Parliament—many of them Puritans—opposed to the absolute power claimed by King Charles I. England's civil war arrived in Maryland in 1644 in the person of Lord Baltimore's old rival, William Claiborne, who fought on the side of the Parliament against the king.

Claiborne seized St. Marys City in 1645.

To support his claim to Maryland, Claiborne made an alliance with Richard Ingle, a reckless and renegade ship captain. Early in 1645 they seized St. Marys City. Claiborne returned to claim his former home and trading post on Kent Island. Maryland now had two opposing rulers: Governor Calvert, ruling the colony through the royal charter of his brother, Lord Baltimore, and the troublesome Claiborne, who held the capital city by force.

In December 1646 Governor Calvert marched on St. Marys and recaptured the city. But when Calvert died on June

9, 1647, Claiborne and Ingle saw their second chance. They stockpiled arms, denounced the proprietor and his royal charter, and prepared their own council to rule the colony.

To gain support among the colonists, Lord Baltimore appointed a Protestant, William Stone, as the new governor of Maryland. Stone ordered defenses to be raised at St. Marys and appointed Protestants as a majority on the governor's council. Peace and order gradually returned to Maryland. To allow the colonists a voice in their own affairs, Lord Baltimore called a meeting of an assembly in 1649. The assembly included twenty-one landowners and four colonial officials.

Toleration in Maryland

In 1649 the parliamentary forces scored a victory over King Charles I. The king was captured, sentenced to death, and beheaded. The kingdom of England was transformed into the Commonwealth of England—a republic governed by a committee of Parliament and by the Puritan leader Oliver Cromwell.

Protestants had also gained the upper hand in Maryland. But all of the Maryland colonists saw the danger of further feuding in North America. They had not risked death at sea and hunger in the New World to fight with fellow colonists over religion. Lord Baltimore himself wanted to attract as many settlers—Anglican, Puritan, Quaker, or Catholic—as he could to Maryland. He also wanted to protect Catholic settlers in case the Protestants grew to form a large majority in the colony.

The result was the Act Concerning Religion, which the proprietor approved and which the Maryland Assembly passed on April 21, 1649. This act, also known as the Toleration Act, allowed all Protestant sects as well as Catholics to freely practice their religion within Maryland. It read, in part, "No person or persons whatsoever within this Province ... Professing to believe in Jesus Christ, shall from henceforth bee any waies [ways] troubled, molested or discountenanced for or in respect of his or her religion nor in the free exercise thereof. . . . Nor any way compelled to the beliefe or exercise of any other Religion against his or her consent."[7]

It was the first formal act of religious toleration ever passed in the English-speaking world. But the act also punished non-Christians,

Margaret Brent

Margaret Brent arrived in Maryland in November 1638. A skilled and energetic businesswoman, she realized that the colony held fine opportunities for women, who had little chance for gainful employment in England. She arrived as the head of her own household and, as such, claimed her own grant of land. She loaned money and traded in tobacco. She kept her independence as well: At a time and place when men outnumbered women six to one, she remained unmarried.

Margaret Brent's abilities drew the notice of Governor Calvert. In 1647, from his deathbed, Calvert appointed Brent as the executor of his estate. The assignment was a difficult one: The governor had left large debts, the colonial treasury was empty, and William Claiborne's army of Protestants and privateers were mauling the colony's militia. Brent took swift action, selling some of Lord Baltimore's cattle to pay soldiers loyal to him.

For her ability, Brent sought respect as well as representation. On January 21, 1648, she stood before the Maryland Assembly and demanded the right to vote—the first woman in the colonies to do so. Unfortunately, the assembly denied her request, and Lord Baltimore did not forgive the loss of his cattle. Having lost the support of the proprietor, she moved to Virginia in 1651.

who could suffer fines, whippings, and the death penalty for their beliefs.

The Toleration Act encouraged settlement in Maryland from other colonies—such as Puritan Massachusetts and Anglican Virginia—that did not tolerate rival sects. Soon after it passed, a group of Puritans arrived from Virginia to settle a town named Providence on the Severn River. Other small settlements appeared along the Chesapeake and its tributaries, built by Catholics as well as Protestants seeking a haven to practice their religion in peace. The idea of religious toleration would have far-reaching consequences, as historian Samuel Eliot Morison describes: "In no Catholic colonial empire—French, Spanish, or Portuguese—were Protestants allowed to exist, much less to acquire land and hold office. In Maryland . . . there grew up a system of legal religious toleration which became one of the cornerstones of the American republic."[8]

The Fight for Maryland

Religious toleration in Maryland did little to ease religious persecution in the other colonies. Nor did it settle the disputes over who owned and operated Maryland. On the strength of his ties to the Puritan leader Oliver Cromwell, William Claiborne would continue his challenge to Maryland's Catholic proprietor.

In 1652 Claiborne returned to the Chesapeake. He demanded that Governor Stone submit to his authority in Maryland. Stone refused. He may have been a Protestant, but he firmly supported the right of Lord Baltimore to rule his colony.

Claiborne asked for help from the English Parliament. By this time Parliament was firmly in control, and Oliver Cromwell held absolute right of his own as England's Puritan dictator. In 1654 Parliament ordered Lord Baltimore to give up control of the colony. It also ordered Governor Stone to resign his position, and it decreed that Catholics in Maryland no longer had the right to vote. The Maryland Assembly passed a second Act Concerning Religion, one that did not tolerate the Roman Catholic faith.

Lord Baltimore regained control in 1657, when Oliver Cromwell finally recognized his legal authority over Maryland. Claiborne returned to England, and in 1658 Lord Baltimore reinstated the Toleration Act of 1649.

A Campaign for the Delaware

Most Marylanders heard the fighting and debate at St. Marys only as a faint echo, brought by the rumors and information of friends and neighbors who had visited the capital city. Most of Maryland remained a thickly wooded wilderness, where claims had to be won through the hard work of clearing, planting, and cultivating the land. As the problems of England continued, more refugees of the civil war arrived in the woods to settle new estates granted by Lord Baltimore.

As these new settlers arrived, open land grew scarce. The Maryland colony began to test its own boundaries. Surveyors ventured east from the Chesapeake to explore the land between the bay and the Delaware River. Their task was to claim for Maryland all of the land stretching west to the Delaware River. But there was one important hurdle to overcome. According to the original charter granted to Lord Baltimore, his colony included only unsettled land, and small settlements had existed along the Delaware well before the arrival of the *Ark* and the *Dove* at St. Clements Island.

Lord Baltimore had good reasons for wanting the land. At its mouth, the Delaware River widened into a broad bay that made it easy for merchant ships to reach the Delaware River settlements. Any colony that controlled the western shore would also control a busy and convenient route to the interior, where fur traders carried on a profitable business. In England, Lord Baltimore pressed his claims to the Delaware with the king, while the Maryland Assembly established Durham County on the western shore of the Delaware.

But English, Swedish, Finnish, and Dutch settlers had been living along the Delaware for decades, turning it into a stew of contesting settlements. As the Maryland Assembly expected, Lord Baltimore's claim was contested. In 1664 King Charles II granted the Delaware region to his brother James, duke of York, an heir to the English throne. In 1673 Charles Calvert, the son of Lord Baltimore, decided to fight for his claim to the Delaware. He commissioned a militia under the command of

Trouble in Maryland

Although Lord Baltimore's colony was intended to be a place of religious tolerance, disputes did arise between Protestants and Catholics in Maryland. The first on record took place in 1638, when the Protestant servants of William Lewis, a Catholic, charged Lewis with proselytizing his faith. For this offence, Lewis was fined five hundred pounds of tobacco.

A more serious case arose three years later, when Thomas Gerard was charged with stealing the keys of the chapel shared by Protestants and Catholics in St. Marys. Gerard was also accused of removing Protestant books from the chapel. He was found guilty and was ordered to pay the customary fine of five hundred pounds of tobacco, which was held in trust to pay the salary of the first Protestant minister to arrive in Maryland.

Captain Thomas Howell, who marched eastward, capturing and burning a Dutch town. The fighting continued for several years. English and Dutch soldiers campaigned up and down the Delaware valley, burning villages, capturing ferries and merchant ships, and making life miserable for the settlers. Finally, the duke of York decided to rid himself of this nuisance. In 1682 he granted the western side of the Delaware to the Quaker William Penn, the proprietor of the vast colony lying north of Maryland known

William Penn gained control of the western side of the Delaware in 1682.

as Pennsylvania. Lord Baltimore's claim to the Delaware was denied because, as the king's ministers pointed out, the territory had been inhabited before the granting of the Maryland charter. The seeds were sown for a long and bitter debate between Maryland and Pennsylvania over the boundary that separated the two colonies.

Instead of rallying Maryland to Lord Baltimore's defense, the border disputes with Pennsylvania caused further dissension within Maryland. As historian J. A. Doyle describes it, "The colonization of Pennsylvania had also a detrimental influence on the position of Baltimore. Boundary disputes sprang up in which he was necessarily opposed to Penn. This told against Baltimore in more ways than one. In the first place, it cannot have failed to alienate from him the Quaker settlers in his own colony."[9]

The difficult job of governing an unruly colony exasperated the third Lord Baltimore. In 1683 he decided to leave Maryland for good and return to England. Although the proprietorship would remain hereditary, Lord Baltimore preferred the more comfortable world of London to the turbulence and rough living of the colonial frontier. In his absence, however, the disputes between loyal supporters and the Country Party, and between Protestants and Catholics, grew worse.

Colonists and Indians

At the same time, as the settlers moved inland, friction with Native Americans began. In search of unclaimed land, the colonists gradually moved up the Potomac River and into the surrounding mountains. Indians saw their land and their hunting grounds fast disappearing.

Both sides carried out the violence. The Indians gathered small war parties to attack isolated farmhouses, burning the thin-walled homes and stables and murdering those who had not fled. The whites fought back by rounding up militia, marching upstream and into the woods, and destroying all Indian villages in their path.

For many years, the war remained a stalemate. There was plenty of room to run on both sides and not enough weapons or combatants on either for a decisive victory. But the Indians found there was one enemy they could not fight: the many diseases carried by the European settlers. Because these diseases were new to North America, the natives had no immunity to them. For the Indians, smallpox, influenza, pneumonia, cholera, typhoid, and yellow fever all were deadly sicknesses that could not be cured. The epidemics raced through the Maryland woods and along the tributaries of the Chesapeake, brought by contagious traders and farmers. Entire villages disappeared when the survivors moved away, relocating to the western mountains, where they believed they would be safe from the settlers and their diseases.

Still, the Indians were not ready to abandon the valley of the Potomac. They raided homes, crops, and livestock on both sides of the river. In retaliation, the settlers marched on Indian villages, rarely making the distinction between hostile and friendly Indians. In 1675 full-scale war broke out. Murders on both sides of the river prompted Virginia and Maryland to call up militias and order a campaign to destroy hostile Indians. The colonies organized temporary militias, five-hundred–strong units of armed citizens. The Maryland governor's council placed one such force under the command of Major Thomas Truman.

Truman marched his men to a Susquehannock fort at the mouth of the Piscataway River. To break a long standoff, Truman agreed to meet with a delegation of Indians. He promised that any Susquehannock who came forward to negotiate would not be harmed. Five

Susquehannock leaders accepted the offer and walked across the open ground to the militia camp. But a party of Virginians, enraged at the murder of a group of peaceful farmers, killed the five Susquehannock.

The militias then laid siege to the fortress. The siege lasted seven weeks, and more than fifty militia members lost their lives. The siege ended as the weather grew cold and the Potomac River froze. Under cover of night, the surviving Susquehannock left their fort and crossed the river to safety in the forests and mountains of Virginia.

The days of hunting and farming north of the Potomac soon came to an end for the Native Americans. By the end of the seventeenth century, settlers had moved farther west, and the Indians had fled before them. Land reserved for Native Americans, either by promise or by treaty, was sold to white settlers. Only a few scattered survivors would remain in Lord Baltimore's territory.

Religious Rivalries

The whites and the Indians never did manage to live together, nor would the Protestants and Catholics forget their differences. In the 1680s rumors of a plot against the king began spreading in England. Events came to a climax in 1688, the year of what some in England called the Glorious Revolution. The Catholic King James II was overthrown by William of Orange, a Dutch Protestant. In Maryland, the colonists heard rumors of a massacre of Protestants by the Catholics as well as an invasion of the colony by the Catholic loyalists. In July 1689 Protestant insurgents staged an attack on the proprietor's official residence in St. Marys. The inhabitant of the house, Governor Quarry, surrendered. In the meantime, Protestants were seizing control of the local county governments.

Catholic King James II was overthrown during the Glorious Revolution.

Protestants held the reins in every county except Ann Arundel, as Doyle explains: "That county, we are more than once told, was now the richest and most important in the colony, and it is possible that increasing prosperity had dulled the edge of religious zeal."[10]

With the accession of William and his queen, Mary, in England, the Protestants saw a chance for a fundamental change in Maryland: the end of proprietary control. The opposing parties—the Country Party and the Loyalists, who sided with Lord Baltimore—sent separate pleas to the new king. The Catholics argued for keeping the proprietary system, and the Protestant party argued for the overthrow of the proprietor and establishment of a Crown colony, meaning direct control of Maryland by the king.

The Maryland revolutionaries also established a convention—that is, a special session of representatives who would decide on fundamental changes in the law. It was the first such convention ever assembled in the North American colonies. The members rose to deliver their complaints against Lord Baltimore: that he was interfering with the courts and the assembly, that he was imposing illegal duties and taxes on the colonists, and that he had no regard for the colony's settlers.

King William heard the complaints against Lord Baltimore and acted. The sovereignty of the proprietors over Maryland abruptly ended. Although the proprietors would still have the right to collect quitrents from the Maryland settlers, the colony itself now belonged to the Crown. As a Crown colony, Maryland would be administered by officials appointed by the king.

In that year, royal power reached its zenith in the colony when the Anglican Church was established as Maryland's official church. Colonial officials took their directions directly from the king of England and worked in concert with Anglican clergy, who were to be appointed by the governors.

The Proprietor Returns

The governors who ran Maryland as a Crown colony did not resolve the many conflicts within the colony, nor did they manage without strong opposition. They were in constant dispute with the Puritan settlers, who believed that sovereignty rested not with royal officials but with the members of their congregations. (To the Puritans, the congregation of the church defined the social, political, and religious community in which they lived. The governors found themselves at odds with Marylanders who worked for the proprietor as collectors of taxes and duties. They also had trouble with settlers who saw Maryland as a refuge from the absolute rule of England's king and his tyrannical officials.

Benedict Leonard Calvert, the fourth Lord Baltimore, saw which way the winds were blowing. In this new England of Protestant and Anglican power, there was simply no way a Roman Catholic would be allowed the same rights enjoyed by the first proprietor. In his quest to regain control of Maryland, Lord Baltimore converted to Protestanism. In 1715 the colony's proprietary government was restored—with strict limitations. Doyle points out, "Though the Proprietor was formally restored, his position was changed. The interval of twenty years had broken the spell of personal influence, nor was any sentiment of loyalty likely to revive when its object was an obscure youth who had never set foot in the colony." [11]

For the rest of its history as a colony, Maryland would remain the property of a distant Englishman, titled Lord Baltimore, a descendant of George and Cecilius Calvert and a loyal servant of the English king.

In the meantime, the economy of Maryland was undergoing important changes. The colony had long depended on the export of tobacco to England, but that business was faltering. As prices rose and then fell, growers unable to make a profit at tobacco growing suffered uncertainty and in some cases financial ruin. The result was a transformation to a more diverse economy, which affected nearly every aspect of daily life in Maryland.

Chapter Three

Daily Life in Colonial Maryland

The tobacco economy had a strong influence on the daily lives of the colonial Marylanders, from the poorest indentured servant to the wealthiest landholder. But tobacco was a fragile foundation for a growing colony's economy. The failure of the tobacco market, beginning in the late seventeenth century, brought about economic diversification in the early 1700s, when Maryland's first cities were founded and new industries were developed. Still, Maryland remained rural and agricultural, and farming was the way of life for most Marylanders until the time of the American Revolution.

Hard Work in a New Country

Maryland's earliest European settlers lived along the lower reaches of Chesapeake Bay and the northern shore of the Potomac River. The waterways for the colonists provided an easy way to transport their crops to the colony's trading posts. They could obtain supplies from the passing ships of traders and merchants. If necessary, they could escape down the river to the sheltering palisades of St. Marys.

For the people of England, the Chesapeake Bay presented an inviting opportunity. The people who settled there and made up Chesapeake society were, in the words of historian Jack Green, competitive, exploitive, and very heavily devoted to commercial agricultural production for an export market. Its high demand for labor and high mortality rates combined to produce a population that was disproportionately male, young, single, immigrant, and mobile. The process of family formation was slow. Social institutions were weak, authority was tenuous, and individualism was strong.[12]

As new ships arrived from England, the line of settlement moved to the west and the north. The settlers cleared their small acreages, breaking the soil, planting grain or small plots of tobacco, and grazing small herds of sheep and cattle.

Maryland farmers were practical and hardworking individuals who had to provide themselves with most of life's essentials. As Matthew Page Andrews relates,

Lumber mills were built from trees hewn on the spot, and the wheels were sometimes made entirely by hand. . . . Leather

Most of Maryland's earliest settlers were farmers, who cultivated fields close to Maryland's waterways so they could easily transport their crops to the colony's trading posts.

was tanned and used for footwear. Wool and flax were woven by the women and servants into commercial articles of coarse grade. Wheat was grown for export; also flax seed, and hemp; while bales of sassafras roots seem to have found a wide sale in the markets of Europe. [13]

A few small villages existed in Maryland, but most settlers lived on land they cleared in the countryside. The forests provided abundant building material; stones collected from the fields made strong foundations. Their homes were rectangular, and many had two stories under a sloping, gabled roof. The most common side walls were brick, whereas the front and back walls consisted of a frame of sawed logs covered with wooden planks. The builder poured rubble and broken bricks within the walls to insulate the house from the wind and cold. A fireplace built into one of the side walls provided heat for the house as well as a place for cooking. On larger estates, the owner built the kitchen in a small side building, which also held supplies of food, tools, utensils, and lumber.

The settlers furnished their houses with simple beds, benches, cupboards, and tables. They ate from bowls and plates made of wood or from fired clay. The dirt floors were pressed smooth and swept; in time, the owner built a floor of rough wooden planks, fastened into the hard soil with round pegs.

Within the clearing and near the home, the settlers constructed small outbuildings. Stables sheltered horses and draft animals. Sheep and pigs were kept in crude wooden pens, and sheds kept harvested crops out of the weather. Smokehouses were used for curing and preserving meat. Farmers who grew grain also built small mills to grind wheat, barley, and oats into flour.

There was little leisure time for men and women. According to archaeologist Anne Elizabeth Yentsch, "Women also worked in the fields. Since tobacco was labor-intensive, there was little time for anything else; Chesapeake housewives rarely had time to spin and weave, to sew and cook. The simplest foods, coarse and meager, sufficed; the plainest clothes made do." [14]

It was common for men as well as women to suffer from poor health, poverty, homesickness, and loneliness. There was little time to

Women worked alongside men on tobacco plantations and rarely had time for leisurely pursuits.

dwell on one's problems, however, as mere survival demanded hard work—from the very first day one arrived on the small acreage that would become home.

The Tobacco Trade

When setting out their new estates, Maryland's farmers sought level, fertile land that could be easily cleared of rocks and trees. They raised wooden fences, usually of split logs, to separate their land from that of their neighbors. Boundary stones also served to mark one's private frontier.

The climate was mild, and the soil of eastern Maryland was loamy and fertile. One strange little plant, native to North America, grew especially well here: the sot weed, or tobacco. In hopes of profiting from tobacco export, the wealthiest Maryland landowners built large plantations overlooking the Potomac and other major rivers. During the seventeenth century, these plantations made tobacco the principal cash crop of Maryland. Because tobacco was in high demand in England, where climate and soil prevented farmers from growing it,

When They Were Young

There were few spoiled children in colonial Maryland. Most families could only provide their children with the bare necessities, as recounted by Maryland historian Lorena S. Walsh quoted in Thad W. Tate and David L. Ammerman, The Chesapeake in the Seventeenth Century:

Since most houses were quite small, usually just one or two rooms, children generally slept with their brothers and sisters in the same room as their parents or in a loft above. Most children were provided with but one new suit of clothes and a pair of shoes and stockings per year. They might in addition be given combs, and boys perhaps received pocket knives. There was little in a typical merchant's stock that was designed specifically for the young, aside from clothing....

Usually the only valuable thing children possessed was livestock. Frequently a father would register a separate livestock mark for each child, and when his stock gave birth he would present the child with an animal of his own. Grandparents, uncles and aunts, and godparents might also give a favorite child livestock. Gifts of animals were the seventeenth-century equivalent of opening a bank account or purchasing a savings bond for a child today.

the tidewater region of Maryland and Virginia held a valuable monopoly. Tobacco money allowed a few Maryland planters to buy slaves and hire servants, build livestock herds, acquire land, and build mansions. Tobacco furnished their homes with luxuries: fine furniture imported from Europe, silver and glass, oil paintings, musical instruments, and rugs and tapestries. Historian Charles Albro Barker describes the tobacco society: "In the eighteenth century the influence of the tobacco staple was felt at every level and in every area of Maryland life. Slaves and servants cultivated it; landholders had their fortunes in it; officials received their salaries in it; it was widely, although not exclusively, used as a medium of exchange." [15]

But tobacco proved a tough taskmaster for those who actually did the work of growing it. Tobacco needed well-drained and fertile land.

The plant also demanded nitrogen, potash, and other nutrients. After a few years of cultivation, it exhausted the soil in which it grew. For this reason, tobacco plantations kept much of their land untouched, held in reserve for future clearing. Tobacco growers had to conserve the forests they owned for harvesting lumber used for drying sheds and for the casks used to transport their crop to market.

Above all, tobacco required long hours, every day, of backbreaking labor. Tobacco farmers first had to prepare seed beds by hoeing and weeding the soil. They set the tiny seeds into the ground by hand, then covered the seeds with straw or cloth to protect them from the cold. As the plants grew, they were pruned to prevent them from branching. This pruning allowed the individual leaves of each plant to grow as large as possible. Weeding the plants and removing parasites and worms from the leaves took up the long and hot days of summer and early fall.

After being cut, tobacco leaves were allowed to wilt in the field and then were brought to a drying shed. The farmers carefully separated the leaves by their quality and size and packed them into small wooden barrels known as hogsheads. Carts drawn by horses or mules brought the barrels from the shed to the nearest ferry, which shipped the product to a merchant.

Tobacco, one of colonial Maryland's principal crops, was a labor-intensive plant, requiring long hours of strenuous cultivation.

For everyone involved, tobacco was a tricky, time-consuming business. As one member of the Calvert family described it in a letter to Lord Baltimore, "In Virginia and Maryland Tobacco is our staple, is our All, and indeed leaves no room for anything Else; It requires the Attendance of all our hands, and Exacts their utmost labour, the whole year around; it requires us to abhor Communities or townships, since a Planter cannot Carry on his Affairs, without Considerable Elbow room, within his plantation." [16]

Tobacco growing tended to isolate farmers, who rarely found the time or the means to travel far from their homes and fields. Few towns existed, and the lack of strong communities made colonial Maryland an often harsh and lonely place. Men and women had to rely on themselves for the necessities of life and might search in vain for any emotional support or sympathy from others. Contributing to the problem was a lack of strong family ties. According to Lorena S. Walsh, "Most had come as indentured servants, and even among the free immigrants there were few family groups. When the immigrants left

---

The Most Famous Joke in Colonial Maryland

During the 1730s the hardy and stubborn Marylander Thomas Cresap fought hard for land he claimed along the Susquehanna River in northern Maryland. Cresap's campaign ended when he was taken prisoner and was brought north to a Philadelphia jail. His capture brought about a well-known one-liner that was recorded as one of the finest displays of wit in colonial Maryland. Carl Bode retells the story in Maryland: A Bicentennial History.

When the sheriff demanded his surrender—we still have the sheriff's report— "Cresap, with several horrid oaths and the most abusive language against the Proprietor and people of Pennsylvania, answered that they should never have him till he was a corpse." They did have him, however, after setting fire to his log house. Shackled, he was marched through the streets of Philadelphia to jail. Along the way he gibed to one of the guards, "Damn it, Aston, this is one of the prettiest towns in Maryland."

Europe, their break with their families was usually complete. Few of them expected ever to return to the Old World, and probably there was little communication with relatives left behind."[17]

One group of Marylanders suffered the most, as they were treated by the settlers not as individuals but as property. These were the slaves, whose numbers in Maryland steadily rose throughout the colonial period. Their lives were brutal and usually short; they were torn from their families for good, and they had no chance—by the laws of the king and of the colony—of attaining independence or gaining any voice in their own affairs.

Slaves and Tobacco

To cultivate their tobacco fields, landowners needed workers. At first, indentured servants met this demand. The indentured servants worked long days and lived in tiny, dark, drafty wooden cabins built on the plantation land. They survived on gritty cornmeal, thin porridge, flour biscuit, and, when times and the hunting were good, meat cooked fresh or preserved in smoke and brine. Along with poor diet and poor sanitation, they fell victim to injuries, exhaustion, and hunger. They could be whipped by their owners for talking back, for missing work, or for working too slowly. They were also susceptible to the many diseases that had driven the Indians away: smallpox, typhoid, pneumonia, and malaria, a common disease in the marshy lands near the rivers. Most of their infant children died, sometimes on the same day they were born.

Most indentured servants lived short lives, and many of them died before their term of service ended. Yet they were vital to the colony, as James Horn relates: "These newcomers fulfilled two vital functions: they provided the labor necessary for the production of the colonies' staple, tobacco, and they replenished a declining population that was unable to reproduce itself by natural means until the last quarter of the century. Without sustained immigration, the Chesapeake colonies would have failed."[18]

As the tobacco economy of Maryland grew, a shortage of labor developed as well. The end of the civil and religious wars of England also shortened the supply of indentured English servants, who found ample opportunity as the economy improved in the home country.

Maryland landowners brought slaves from Africa to cultivate their tobacco fields and to sustain their economy.

Many Maryland planters saw only one solution to the problem: Africans. There had been Africans in the colony since the arrival of the *Ark*, which carried Maryland's first African colonist, Matthias de Sousa. Most of the Africans who followed de Sousa had been slaves, but some had been free, and both groups were greatly outnumbered by indentured servants. By the late seventeenth century, however, tobacco, along with the slaves who grew and cultivated it, had become a mainstay of the Maryland economy, and the slave trade had become a vital part of daily life along Chesapeake Bay.

At this time, English and Dutch slave merchants were carrying out a three-way business between Europe, Africa, and North America. They brought European goods to the western coast of Africa, where the goods were traded for human beings. Many of their African captives were prisoners of war or had been taken on a slaving expedition carried out by either Europeans or Africans. (The tribes of western Africa did not hesitate to kidnap their rivals and exchange them with the Europeans for goods they lacked.)

The captives were chained and brought aboard slaving ships, where they were held belowdecks like cattle in a livestock pen. Many died of hunger, thirst, and disease even before they reached North America. Those who survived were either brought ashore to be auctioned to the highest bidder or sold from the deck while the ship anchored in port.

For the African slave in the colonies, there was no returning home and no chance for freedom. Maryland passed laws harshly punishing those who tried to run away. By a law passed in 1664, even slaves who were baptised as Christians could not be free. Any African brought to Maryland would be a slave for his or her entire life. The Maryland slaveowners also wanted to guard against another danger: intermarriage between whites and blacks. A law of 1664 made any white woman who married an African man a servant of the African's master for the rest of her life.

To regulate the trade in slavery, the English government passed the Act to Regulate the Negroes on the British Plantations in 1667. This law put strict controls on the lives of the slaves. They could not leave their plantation on Sundays, when most were given a day of rest. (During the rest of the week, they could leave only with a pass issued by their owners.) The slaves could own no weapons, nor could they own any musical instruments. Slaveowners did not want their slaves using horns, drums, or other instruments to communicate with each other and possibly signal an escape or a rebellion. The act of 1667 also established whipping as the punishment for the crime of striking a white. For a second such offense, the slave's face could be branded with a hot iron.

The importation of slaves had a long-lasting effect on the plantation economy of Maryland. As historian Aubrey C. Land describes it, "Alongside the familiar family plantation ... emerged the great planter. Owner of a dozen to a score of servile laborers, he set a new lifestyle based on landholdings larger than anything previously known. ... Slaves and land were the conspicuous signs of the new elite." [19]

The Maryland Dollar

The word *dollar* came from a fifteenth-century coin known as the thaler, which was used in the Holy Roman Empire. In the English colonies of North America, the first dollars were silver coins worth eight Spanish reales (also known as the Spanish dollar). Although Spanish reales dominated trade between the New and Old World, the dollar became the customary unit used in transactions among the different British colonies (each of which also had its own money, based on British sterling).

By the mid–eighteenth century, two different kinds of money existed in Maryland: "proclamation" money and "common" money. Both types had different rates of exchange into the Spanish dollar. In addition, there was "exchange" money, which was used for foreign transactions. For this reason, confusion often reigned when Marylanders attempted to transact business within and outside of their colony.

In 1767 Maryland solved its dilemma by becoming the first colony to set an official denomination of money known as dollars. Its exchange rate was set at four shillings, six pence sterling of British money. The Continental Congress accepted the dollar as the denomination of the paper money in the colonies in 1775, and for the nation's first coins, issued at the Philadelphia mint beginning in 1792.

Perils of the Tobacco Economy

Tobacco planters believed slavery was necessary for their own survival. They had to compete with other growers, who also had the use of slave labor. The margin of profit was slim even in good times, and growers realized that an extra expense, or a bad growing season, could put them out of business for good.

An important reason for this was the cutthroat tobacco market, and the hard-bargaining buyers and traders who worked in Maryland's river ports. These buyers made life difficult for tobacco growers by perpetrating many tricks and frauds for the sake of a profitable trade with England. The merchants paid low prices for the crop and then sold the goods for much higher prices to English buyers. When the market for tobacco grew soft, and prices declined, the traders simply paid less and the grower suffered the loss.

By the early eighteenth century, the dependence on the tobacco market was making life perilous for many Maryland planters. To protect themselves, some invested in herds of sheep, cattle, and goats. Others experimented with new produce, including grain, fruit orchards, and hemp, which was used in the manufacture of rope. Maryland farmers also found a good business in the milling of flour, which was used to make biscuit for use by the British navy. In their introduction to *Colonial Chesapeake Society*, Lois Green Carr and Philip Morgan comment: "Better-off planters, in particular, added wheat and other grains to their crops and produced cloth, leather, and metal products that earlier they had imported. Hence, local markets began to develop and over time the economy became more diversified and stable."[20]

Some Maryland farmers gave up entirely and moved to the cities to try their luck as tradesmen. As an industrial revolution was turning many English towns into manufacturing centers, ambitious colonists built small factories in North America. Marylanders benefited from a

The failure of the tobacco market in the eighteenth century forced some Marylanders to abandon their tobacco fields and move to the cities to find other work.

rich vein of iron ore that lay in the northern valleys of their colony, as well as from encouragement offered by the colonial assembly. Matthew Page Andrews explains, "The legislature of Maryland in 1719 offered 100 acres of land free to anyone who would set up furnaces and [iron] forges in the province. . . . About 1722 further encouragement was extended to the industry in the exemption of its laborers from work in mending the public roads." [21]

Lord Baltimore's City

To further develop industry and merchant trade, the Maryland assembly founded a new town in 1729. The town lay on a deep, broad harbor where the Patapsco River empties into the western shore of Chesapeake Bay. Nearby were iron ore deposits, good timber, and a

A Furnace Blasts into Action

The iron industry bustled in early Maryland, where iron ore deposits spurred the growth of dozens of small blast furnaces and mills. Historian Frederick Gutheim describes the work in his book The Potomac:

"Against the hillside stood the blast furnace, where it could be readily charged from the top with wagonloads of ore, charcoal, and lime. Huge bellows, often driven by water power, built up the necessary heat. In front, on the lower level, was the casting house where the molten iron was poured. Here pig iron, pots, kettles, stove plates, firelocks, and similar articles were cast. Often that was all. The big house of the ironmaster and the smaller cottages of the workers completed the picture. . . .

In favorable situations ironworks grew more complex. Then the pig iron was heated again until it became soft, and beaten out by water-driven trip hammers to make a more refined iron bar for blacksmiths. Often the smiths would set up close to the furnace, and make their tools, locks, implements, and other articles. A further development was the bloomery forge, where more heating and hammering made wrought iron, or the rolling and slitting mills, where iron plates and nails were manufactured."

Maryland colonists lay out the city of Baltimore, founded in 1729 to develop industry and merchant trade.

belt of rich farmland that ran through Maryland and southern Pennsylvania.

In the new city, named in honor of Maryland's proprietor, the first factories produced farming tools such as hoes and plows as well as kitchen utensils. A shipbuilding industry developed, and by the early 1730s a sea of masts decorated Baltimore's crowded docks and harbor. The fast-growing city became a center of iron production. The Baltimore Iron Works turned out pig iron, which was to be fashioned into hoops for barrels, iron fittings for ships, rims for carriage wheels, nails, utensils, needles, and tools. The Baltimore Iron Works became one of the principal manufacturing concerns in the North American colonies.

Maryland's small factories did a brisk business. But in the countryside, many landowners still lived a hard existence. There was little money circulating in the colony, and landowners needed money to make improvements on their properties. Some broke up their plantations and sold parcels to new settlers and to former indentured servants. The head-right system, which had granted land outright to new arrivals based on the size of their households, ended in 1683. After this date, anyone arriving to settle in Maryland had to pay money or tobacco for new land.

It began to dawn on Maryland's settlers that they did not live in a limitless expanse of land, free for the taking and ready for the plow and the hoe. Open land was disappearing fast, and the frontier reached only so far as the Blue Ridge Mountains. Beyond these hills, and past the sources of the Potomac and the Shenandoah Rivers, hostile Indian tribes made settlement nearly suicidal.

Another factor was at play on the frontier: the clash of England and France for control of the Great Lakes region, the Ohio River valley, and the Appalachian Mountains. This clash would continue through the middle of the eighteenth century. Although it would be won by the English, the costs in both money and blood were high. The king of England demanded help from his North American colonists, in the form of new taxes on goods and duties on trade. The colonists, in turn, began demanding their rights for representation as ordinary citizens of the king. The contest between king and colonists would lead to a loud cry for independence, war with the king's soldiers, and the end of the Maryland colony.

Chapter Four

The Revolution in Maryland

Although the proprietor's rights were restored in 1715, the fourth Lord Baltimore enjoyed little support or sympathy among the members of the colony. The colonists concluded that this proprietor cared very little about their welfare—after all, he had not even set foot in his own colony. The disputes between the authorities—both English and proprietary—and the Marylanders continued, growing more bitter. Eventually, these conflicts united the people of Maryland against not only the proprietor but also the king and the English government.

Disenchantment with England

The people of Maryland felt their loyalty to England grow strained as the king and his ministers continued to treat them as nothing more than a useful source of goods and trade. William Hand Browne comments: "The colonists owed their prosperity, under Providence, to nothing but their own resolution and industry, and England . . . only meddled with them to despoil them of their territory, to hamper their commerce for her advantage, or to demand their money for her treasury, leaving them, in other matters, to sink or swim as best they could." [22]

Across the Atlantic Ocean, the English felt little concern for disputes over land and authority, for heavy taxes and duties, for shady tobacco merchants, or for the danger of Native Americans on the frontier. English merchants, and the king, looked on the colonies as a resource. The fields, forests, and mines of North America supplied the mother country with goods that it needed. These goods—raw materials such as lumber and wool—were sent across the ocean for the use of English manufacturers. In turn, England sold finished goods—such as furniture and clothing—back to the colonies.

This system of mercantilism made the North American colonists dependent on England. The tobacco growers, merchants, and shipbuilders of Maryland did well only as long as England prospered. They saw their luck grow hard when the English economy slowed down. All the time, they paid import duties on goods arriving from overseas. They had no way to prevent or protest these taxes—no one represented them in the king's government or in Parliament. They were free citizens with very few rights.

Much smaller and more sparsely populated than its neighbors Pennsylvania and Virginia, Maryland also depended on England for its defense. As settlement reached farther west into the Appalachian Mountains, the colonists ran into powerful Indian tribes as well as French trappers and fur traders arriving from the north. Defending England's claims in North America grew difficult, dangerous, and increasingly expensive. As the raids and violence continued, the colonists had to organize militias. Members of the militias had to equip themselves with muskets, lead shot, and gunpowder. These militiamen lost time and money, and sometimes their lives, by marching and fighting in the wilderness. Many colonists began to complain about the poor protection the king was giving them.

Trouble on the Frontier

Occasional trouble with Indians on the frontier developed into a state of war by the 1750s. The two most powerful empires in the world, England and France, both claimed land in North America. In this fight, the French enlisted the help of several powerful Indian nations. For this reason, the fighting that took place in North America in the 1750s and early 1760s is known as the French and Indian Wars.

Mason and Dixon

Maryland reached its truce with the colony of Pennsylvania in 1760, when the rival colonies agreed to hire two English surveyors, Charles Mason and Jeremiah Dixon. Mason and Dixon were to decide, once and for all, the disputed borders between Maryland, Delaware, and Pennsylvania.

The surveyors arrived in 1763 and immediately went to work. Starting in the east, they marched in a ruler-straight line, following a latitude of 30 degrees, 43 minutes, and 17.6 seconds north of the equator. A company of lumberjacks walked the line with them, cutting a swath of trees to create a clear corridor along the boundary. After 233 miles of hard progress, Mason and Dixon halted, facing hostile Indians to the west. Eventually, in 1769, Maryland and Pennsylvania agreed to the Mason-Dixon Line as their common border. Much later the line would represent something more important: the boundary between South and North, slave state and free state.

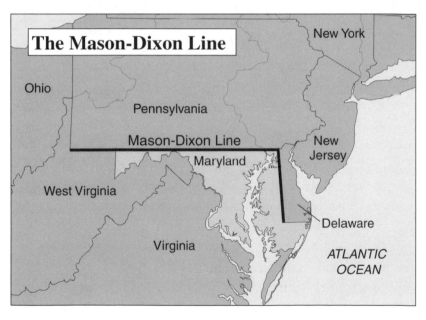

The tide of the French and Indian Wars eventually turned in England's favor. In 1763 the French agreed to the Treaty of Paris, which awarded England nearly all of France's North American territories. Fearing for the future safety of his valuable colonies, the king signed the

The struggle for control of North American territory erupted in war between England and France and their Native American allies in 1763.

Royal Proclamation in the same year. The proclamation forbade colonial settlement west of the Allegheny Mountains. The British returned their claim to the western territory, as far as the Mississippi River, back to the Indians. The British government felt it could not protect any colonists who risked settling there.

Britain had incurred heavy debts to pay for the French and Indian War. Although the war had been won, the future of the North American colonies looked doubtful. The ministers of the Privy Council, who acted as the king's personal advisers, feared that defending the colonies would drain their country's treasury. There seemed only one fair way to pay for the defense of the colonies: Tax the colonists.

Taxation Without Representation

The English Parliament wasted little time before passing the Revenue Act of 1764, also known as the Sugar Act. This law put duties on coffee, indigo, sugar, and other products imported into the colonies. Colonial merchants who had to pay these duties passed their higher costs on to their customers. For the ordinary colonist in Maryland, imported goods became more and more expensive.

England placed another restriction on the colonists with the Currency Act, which stopped the printing of paper money in the colonies. The ministers feared that colonial currency would make English money worth less. But as a result of the Currency Act, the colonists saw the value of their savings fall. Silver coinage grew scarce, and many people had to barter (trade) for their goods, their homes, and their land. The Sugar Act and the Currency Act had their strongest effects in port cities such as Baltimore and Annapolis, where merchants saw trade and their profits decline.

The colonists grumbled long and loud about the new laws. Not only did the Sugar Act and the Currency Act cause them hardship, but these measures also robbed the colonists of their freedoms. Because they had no representatives in Parliament, the colonists could not fight these acts, except by boycotting (refusing to buy) English goods. Since England used the colonies as an important resource and as an exclusive market for its goods, a boycott represented much more than a protest over taxation. It meant outright rebellion against English control over North America.

The Stamp Act

For many colonists, the final straw came in 1765, when Parliament passed the Stamp Act. This act required the colonists to buy stamps for all printed material, such as legal documents, playing cards, and the imported paper used by newspapers and printing houses. Many colonists fiercely opposed the Stamp Act, even before it was put into effect. As Samuel Eliot Morison writes,

The English colonies . . . found the Stamp Act an easy mark, administered as it was by crown-appointed distributors of embossed paper which could be destroyed. . . . In every continental seaport there were formed a group of middle-class citizens who called themselves "Sons of Liberty." . . . These liberty boys, often disguising themselves as workmen or sailors, coerced distributors into resigning, burned the stamped paper, and incited people to attack unpopular local characters. [23]

Angry colonists review the Stamp Act, a tax on printed materials imposed by English Parliament.

Violent demonstrations broke out in many cities. Tax collectors were chased down, tarred and feathered, and run out of several towns. In Annapolis, Samuel Chase marched at the head of a long column of protesters, who hanged and burned a small effigy of the local tax collector as a climax to their demonstration. While merchants and landowners throughout Maryland called loudly for the repeal of the Stamp Act, the agent responsible for collecting the tax was driven out of the colony altogether. Historian Browne describes the fate of Maryland's own stamp-collector: "Excitement soon mounted to fever heat, and when Mr. Hood, a Marylander, who, while in England, had been appointed stamp-distributor for the Province, arrived at Annapolis, he was received with fierce insult and outrage. He was flogged, hanged, and burned in effigy in several towns. . . . His house in Annapolis was torn down."[24]

The English reacted to the rebellion against the Stamp Act with shock and anger. Why shouldn't the colonists pay a portion of the money needed for their own defense? After all, the people of England had been paying a stamp tax for many years. They paid many other taxes and duties as well. In fact, the people of England paid twenty times the amount of taxes and duties paid by colonists in North America.

The colonists had a simple response: If money were to be raised in the colonies, then the colonists should raise it themselves. The British government turned down this idea. To resolve the dispute, the British repealed the stamp tax in 1766, the year after it passed. But the English Parliament still believed it had a right to tax the colonies. With the Townshend Acts, new duties were established for imported glass, paint, tea, and paper. Another uprising in the colonies persuaded Parliament to cancel these taxes in 1770—except for the tax on tea. In the meantime, the uprisings against British taxes had struck a potent spark of defiance and rebellion among colonists in Maryland and throughout North America.

As a result of this rebellion, the people of Maryland began to see themselves as united with their former rivals in Virginia, Pennsylvania, and the other colonies. They saw that their best chance to overcome England's unfair taxation was to band together with the other colonies. Historian Merrill Jensen describes the result:

The Stamp Act sparked violent demonstrations in many cities by colonists opposed to England's taxation.

Events after 1763 jarred Marylanders loose from concern with their internal affairs. They co-operated with other colonies by re-stating the constitutional theories they had long used against the proprietors, but now turned them against British policies. They organized extra-legal associations and used mob violence to defeat the Stamp Act and to attack the Townshend program. [25]

In reaction to the Stamp Act and the Townshend Acts, the Marylanders agreed on a new policy: nonimportation of English goods. No English products would be allowed into Maryland's ports; the merchants of these ports would be prevented from unloading, storing, or selling any English goods as well.

Nonimportation struck directly at the English economy. It threatened not only merchants in the colonies but manufacturers of goods in the home country as well. By uniting on the policy of nonimportation, the colonists saw very clearly that they were much more than colonists and second-class citizens. They were a vital and very necessary part of the English empire.

Defiance in Maryland

In October 1770 the Maryland Assembly had an important decision to make. The Tobacco Inspection Act of 1747 had expired, and the colony needed a new tobacco inspection law. But writing such a law would not be easy. The law would set down the fees to be collected by agents working for the king and the proprietor. The law also would fix the stipend to be paid to the Anglican clergy. These clergy, who were appointed by the proprietor, collected thirty pounds of tobacco from each parishioner every year, and now they were demanding an increase to forty pounds.

For many Marylanders, the Anglican clergy represented yet another tyrannical aspect of proprietary rule as well as an economic hardship. For the next three years, a hot dispute raged over the issue of limiting the incomes of Anglican clergy and the setting of maximum fees to be collected by the proprietors. The assembly was determined to limit fees not only to the clergy but also those duties collected by proprietary officials, some of whom were getting rich off the collections. On the other side, the governor and the proprietor believed they had the right, by the colonial charter, to set down and collect any and all taxes and duties on the colony's goods. The members of the assembly denied that the proprietor had a right to decree the collection of such duties without their assent.

The Governor Acts

In response to the assembly's defiance, Governor Robert Eden suspended and dissolved the legislature. He then established new fees by proclamation—without the agreement of the assembly. To his opponents, this was taxation without representation, as the fees were set arbitrarily by a proprietary official and not by representatives of the people. This action prompted a quick response, related by Jensen:

When the delegates [of the assembly] returned to their counties, they took a step which would have been unthinkable before the furor of the 1760s: they organized popular associations to enforce tobacco inspection. Once more the ordinary citizens of Maryland were given a chance to take part in political action, and what amounted to economic coercion outside the bounds of law. [26]

After the election of 1773—the last in Maryland's colonial history— the assembly began meeting again. In November the assembly agreed to limit clerical incomes to thirty pounds of tobacco per parishioner and to give each taxpayer the option of paying a tax of four shillings in English money instead of in tobacco.

This did not resolve the problem of taxes and duties. The king's ministers were still determined to draw a fair income, one way or another, from their expensive colonies. They had backed down on the Stamp Act, but by the Tea Act of 1773 the British ordered that British tea be imported directly into the colonies. No longer would colonial merchants act as middlemen in the tea business. Instead, British companies would have a monopoly, and no colonists would profit by the trade.

The Tea Act sparked more outrage and rebellion, supported by a fear of total economic dependence on the mother country. In October 1774 the *Peggy Stewart*, carrying a ton of British tea, was riding at anchor in the harbor of Annapolis. To keep the tea from being unloaded, a group of local men forced Anthony Stewart, the shipowner, to sign a confession. The paper stated that Stewart and the local merchants who had ordered the tea had committed an insult to the liberties of America. The Marylanders ordered Stewart to burn his cargo, but Stewart went further than that. Terrified that he and his family would be attacked by Maryland's extremists, he burned his entire ship.

The Continental Congress

Anger against the English spread quickly through the colonies, from Georgia in the south to the small New England colonies to the north. The rebellion was joined by farmers, merchants, and landowners.

Taxation without representation meant tyranny—the lawless, unjust rule of a king whom nobody elected and who exploited the colonies solely for his own glory and for the money they brought to his royal treasury.

In Maryland rebellion was tempered by loyalty to the crown. Many people in Maryland opposed the drive for independence. Their colony had profited by supplying England with tobacco, iron goods, and ships and naval stores. The common people wanted to remain under the statutes of the English common law, and they saw their interests as the same as England's. They feared independence because it might make the proprietor of Maryland—already the most powerful of all colonial lords—into a tyrant in his own right. The people of Maryland also feared the domination of larger colonies, especially their neighbors Virginia and Pennsylvania.

Colonists express outrage over the Tea Act, England's attempt to establish a monopoly on tea imports into the American colonies.

To work out a common plan against British taxes and regulations, the colonial leaders convened the first Continental Congress in Philadelphia, Pennsylvania, on September 5, 1774. The representatives split into two factions: one for outright rebellion against British rule, the other for remaining within the British empire. Members of the Maryland faction argued for remaining loyal, with certain conditions, to the king.

The British responded to the Continental Congress by doing nothing to meet colonial demands for further liberty. Instead, the British sent troops to occupy rebellious colonial towns such as Boston. In the spring of 1775 British troops confronted a ragtag group of local militia in Lexington, Massachusetts. The colonials defiantly fired on the British troops, and militiamen harried the retreating redcoats all along the road from Lexington to Concord. The colonies had begun their war for independence.

The second Continental Congress convened in May 1775. In the meantime, the debate over independence continued within Maryland. Historian Merrill Jensen writes:

> The Maryland convention denied that it and "the people" of
> Maryland wanted independence in January 1776, and when

The first Continental Congress met in 1774 to address the problem of England's economic oppression of American colonists.

Representatives of the thirteen colonies sign the Declaration of Independence, announcing their break from England.

it adjourned that month, several of its leaders held a secret meeting with Governor Robert Eden to discuss means of bringing about reconciliation with Britain. Eden assured the secretary of state that they were sincere in their "abhorrence" of independence. By spring, however, such men . . . were coming to the reluctant conclusion that independence must be the outcome.[27]

On July 4, 1776, the congress formally ratified the Declaration of Independence. Three Maryland delegates to the Continental Congress—Thomas Stone, William Paca, and John Rogers—voted to adopt the declaration. Independence carried the day, and Maryland joined the twelve other British colonies that had agreed to fight.

The Declaration of Independence meant all-out war with the British. To lead the colonials, the Continental Congress nominated George Washington, a Virginia planter, as commander of the Continental

Army. Washington set himself a near-impossible task: organizing poorly trained and ill-equipped colonials into a disciplined army. In the late summer of 1776, he rushed his army south from Massachusetts to Long Island, to guard the city of New York against a British invasion. As Washington expected, the British landed on Long Island in force. At the Battle of Long Island on August 27, a stubborn line of Maryland troops bravely fought off the redcoats, helping Washington to escape with most of his outnumbered army to Manhattan Island and safety. From their stand on Long Island, the Maryland troops earned the nickname the Old Line, a name that was later applied to the entire state of Maryland as its nickname, the Old Line State.

Meanwhile, in Maryland, Chesapeake Bay provided a vital link for the colonies to the outside world. For this reason, the admirals of the British Navy were ordered to set up a blockade of the bay. Merchants and smugglers worked the waters of the bay and its tributaries at their risk. But a complete blockade of the long and winding river estuaries proved impossible. From the many small harbors along these waterways, Maryland ship captains emerged to raid the British ships. These privateers did a brisk business in arms, food, iron, weapons, and other goods vital to the war effort.

In the meantime, the American Revolution was drawing the support of Europeans opposed to England and to monarchy. These so-called Republicans included the Polish count Casimir Pulaski, who organized his own legion of troops in Baltimore in 1778. Later, an aristocratic French officer, Marquis de Lafayette, followed Pulaski to Maryland, where he gathered troops as well as ammunition, clothing, and food for a campaign against the British. Pulaski and Lafayette found full support in Baltimore, a port where anti-British feeling had run at a fever pitch since the days of the Tea Act and the burning of the *Peggy Stewart.*

The Confederation of Colonies

In November 1777 the Continental Congress adopted the Articles of Confederation, establishing a government for the United States of America. In order to go into effect, the articles had to be ratified by each state. The people of Maryland eagerly supported the American Revolution, but the assembly of Maryland set down certain conditions before its members would agree to the articles. They feared the power of larger states, such as Virginia and Pennsylvania. They did not want these states to have the unbounded right to open up the lands west of the Allegheny mountains. This land, instead, should be held in common by all the people of the future country. Maryland took this stand because, as historian J. R. Pole writes, "Men with interests that seemed insecure in the hands of the new state governments . . . hotly denied the legal claims of those governments over the West. They countered with the assertion that the whole of the western territory had descended to the people of all the states, whose only acknowledged government was the Congress itself." [28]

The members of the assembly realized that larger states opposed them. Yet they held fast for three and a half years. Finally, not wanting their own stubbornness to stall the Revolutionary movement, the assembly agreed to allow its delegates to sign the Articles of Confederation even if Maryland's conditions were not met. The Maryland delegation signed the Articles of Confederation on March 1, 1781.

On October 17 of that year, a British garrison surrendered at the fortress of Yorktown, located on the James River in Virginia. Their largest

The British surrender at Yorktown in 1781 virtually ended the Revolutionary War.

army captured, the British called retreat from the colonies. The fighting was not yet over, however. Up and down the shores of Chesapeake Bay, British loyalists and American patriots fought several bloody battles. The bay became a favorite hunting ground of thieves and sea pirates, as the Maryland newspaper *Journal and Advertiser* reported:

> On the 8th instant [of July] the schooner Greyhound, a beautiful boat laden with Salt, Peas, Pork, Bacon, and some Dry Goods ... was taken in Hooper's Straits by the Renegade-Pirate Joe Whaland. [Skipper] Furnival was plundered of his Money, Watch, Hat and indeed everyThing that the Thieves could lay their Hands on. Mr. Furnival saw several other Bay craft fall into the Fangs of the same Vultures before he was released. [29]

In the halls of the king's government, however, ministers and diplomats saw that carrying on the fight for the colonies was useless. With the Treaty of Paris, signed on September 3, 1783, Great Britain formally recognized the independence of the United States of America.

The thirteen colonies had become the thirteen states. Each state now had a sovereign government, and each state was free to write its own laws and set down regulations of business and trade. But independence did not bring agreement. In Maryland the old parties—the Country Party, the Proprietary Party, and Loyalists—were transformed into two major political factions: Federalist and Republican. The clash of these two parties and the interests they represented brought about new battles for the people of the Old Line State.

Chapter Five

Federalists and Republicans in Maryland

M aryland was no longer the property of the Lords Baltimore. The proprietary colony had become an independent state. The free citizens of the state had the right to carry out business as they wished, without rules, regulations, and instructions from England. The religious toleration fought over since the founding of the colony was now written into the U.S. Constitution, which, by the First Amendment, banned the establishment of any official church. Christians—with sufficient property—could not be denied the right to vote or to sit in the assembly based on their religious beliefs. State law only denied these customary rights of free citizens to the members of other faiths, to women, and to slaves.

The assembly itself was divided into two competing political parties: the Federalists and the Republicans. The Federalist Party could claim to be the party that had brought liberty and independence to the United States. The leading men of the party, including George Washington, had fought and won the American Revolution and had written the founding documents of the United States. In Maryland, the Federalists owned the most popular newspapers, ran the banks,

An Election Scandal in Maryland

Members of the Federalist Party, including George Washington, worried about the outcome of the first legislative election in Maryland. The state had long been evenly divided among Protestants and Catholics, and now it seemed that Republicans and Federalists would also have to share power. Maryland's farmers and small-town citizens supported the Republicans, but the larger cities and business interests generally favored the Federalists.

As it turned out, Washington had little to fear. As described by Jeffrey St. John in Forge of Union/Anvil of Liberty, *the election in Maryland was carefully set up to favor the new president's cause.*

"The Maryland legislature allowed for only seventeen days between passage of its election law and the opening of the polls. The law provided for a State-wide at-large election with six districts. Each voter was entitled to vote for six candidates, one in each district rather than from the voter's district; thus the Federalists effectively neutralized Anti-Federalist voting strength in at least three counties and virtually ensured the sweeping victory that so gratified General Washington."

managed the most important industries, and controlled trade. They were for a strong federal government, which would handle the nation's foreign policy, decide on westward expansion, and set up a central bank. But they did not go unchallenged.

The small farmers, tradesmen, and common people looked to the Republicans, made up of men opposed to the domination of the Federalists. This group had Thomas Jefferson, the third president, as their leading national figure. The Republicans stood for the rights of states to control their own destiny. They were strong in Maryland, a small state that feared domination by much larger and wealthier neighbors to the north and south. But from the Federalist view, the Republicans were not much better than common riffraff, as Roger Butterfield relates: "The Federalists seemed to think there was something monstrously immoral and illegal about this rising opposition. Their cartoons pictured the Republicans as cannibals, drunkards, and pirates." [30]

In Maryland, the contest between Federalist and Republican grew most intense over the issue of trade with England and the continent of Europe. The seaports of Maryland depended heavily on this trade, and the survival of merchants in Baltimore, Annapolis, and smaller ports was at stake. Marylanders knew that decisions made in the new national capital of Washington, D.C.—the land for which Maryland had donated to the federal government—could have a drastic effect along Chesapeake Bay.

In Maryland the new state legislature was dominated by the Republican Party, with the Federalists forming a minority. Whereas the Federalists favored a strong central government, the Republicans wrote and spoke for the opposite: a limited federal government, greater liberties for the individual states, and an alliance with France, which had overthrown its own king in 1789 and established a republic.

One of the most important issues for the legislators was the rapid growth of Baltimore, which worried Marylanders from the rest of the state, who feared the city would dominate. Baltimore's representatives made up a powerful voting bloc in the Maryland state legislature, and they favored their home city when it came time to vote on new laws and trade regulations. To combat this, the system of electing representatives

During the eighteenth century, trade with England was vital to the economy of seaport towns such as Baltimore.

in Maryland was changed in 1790. Instead of elections "at large," in which all of the citizens voted for all of the candidates, the voters of each district could only vote for candidates from their own districts.

Maryland's constitution, which had been adopted in 1776, stated that the right to vote in Maryland depended on the amount of property each citizen owned. Simply to cast a vote required a minimum of fifty acres of land or thirty pounds of money. Maryland delegates had to possess five hundred pounds; senators, one thousand pounds; and the governor had to be worth at least five thousand pounds. About this constitution, writer Carl Bode comments,

> [Maryland's constitution was] shrewdly framed in Annapolis by the wealthy for the wealthy and approved in 1776. Under it you had to own property to vote or hold office—as much as £5,000 if you yearned to be governor. Not that the governor wielded much power; the framers, fearful of a strong executive, hedged him in with a newly devised senate as well as a house of delegates and a council. On the other hand the framers weren't merely jealous oligarchs. For all white-skinned Marylanders they provided a bill of rights with more than forty clauses. [31]

In 1801 Maryland again reformed its voting laws by removing most of the property requirements. These restrictions ended completely in 1810. But women, African Americans—both free and slave—as well as Jews still could not vote in Maryland.

The Business of Maryland

While the debates between Federalists and Republicans raged on in the state capital, most Marylanders went about their lives and business. News traveled slowly, and the conflicts of distant politicians held little interest for Marylanders working their small farms or busy with a trade in a town or city. For many people, the important issue was not Republican against Federalist, or even the United States against Great Britain. Instead, they watched and worried over the rise and fall in market prices for cash crops. A drop in the price for tobacco, for example, could ruin a planter who had borrowed money to buy land, tools, and seed. There was no help for hungry families who could not earn enough to support themselves. Many farmers struggling to make a living had to give up their land to speculators—who always stood ready to buy land cheaply—and move to the city.

Although Maryland was still a rural state, its ports and cities were growing rapidly. In Baltimore, where the population reached about thirty thousand by 1800, small-scale manufacturing flourished. There were iron workshops, watchmakers, glass factories, shipyards, mills, and tanneries. Carpenters, glassmakers, coopers, printers, joiners, blacksmiths, and brewers formed guilds to protect their jobs and wages and to express a united voice in political and social affairs. Busy trade and commerce allowed the founding of the Bank of Maryland and the Bank of Baltimore.

Much of Maryland's success was tied to the export of goods to Europe. Since the 1790s European wars had spurred exports of military goods, ships, arms, and ammunition from Baltimore factories. In 1799 Maryland exported more than $16 million worth of goods. In the early 1800s, when the French leader Napoléon campaigned across central Europe, Maryland again benefited from exports, especially to Great Britain, which was fighting Napoléon on land and blockading French ports with a powerful navy.

The state had its share of economic and social problems. One of the smallest states in the Union, Maryland did not produce enough food to support its population, which reached 319,728 by the first national census of 1790. The state had to import its food from other states and from abroad. At the same time, tobacco farming in the tidewater region had exhausted the soil, and erosion was ruining much of the most fertile land bordering the rivers. Most of Maryland's landowners had very few other trades to ply. Unable to keep up their homes and support their households, thousands of them divided and sold the colonial land grants.

Maryland ship captains profited from the conflicts in Europe by privateering and by running the English and French blockades. A privateer was a ship captain who captured enemy cargoes for his own benefit. He held the authority to do this through a letter of marque, a document issued by the American government. But privateering carried risks: Ships could be seized, and their cargoes could be confiscated and,

Benjamin Banneker

In 1753 a young, free African American living in the Oella region of Maryland borrowed a pocket watch from one of his neighbors. The young man promised to return the watch, but first he wanted to carry out a little project.

Benjamin Banneker brought the watch home to his workbench. He carefully removed its cover and dissected its tiny wheels, gears, and springs. He made drawings of each component, then returned the watch to its worried owner; the instrument ran perfectly. Meanwhile, Banneker carved a large wooden clock from his drawings and calculations. The clock struck every hour, on the hour, for the next fifty years.

In 1791 Banneker's skill at mathematics carried him to the notice of the new federal government. He was commissioned to help survey the federal district, which lay along the Potomac River and which would become Washington, D.C.

Two years earlier, at the age of fifty-eight, Banneker had taken up astronomy. Observing the sky with a small telescope, he worked out the times of future solar and lunar eclipses. He published *Benjamin Banneker's Almanac* between 1792 and 1797.

Benjamin Banneker's life and talents proved that, when given their opportunity, African Americans had intelligence and ability equal to that of the European colonists. It was this argument that helped to persuade the framers of the U.S. Constitution to take a modest act against slavery and to ban the importation of slaves twenty years from the signing of the document.

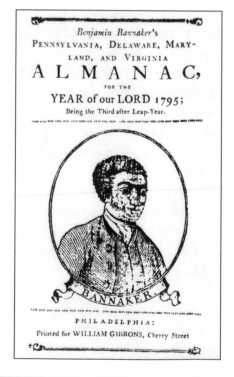

Benjamin Banneker's picture appears on this 1795 edition of his Almanac.

their sailors impressed (forced) into duty in the British navy. Privateering also angered the British, who counted on their blockade to ruin France economically and destroy Napoléon's ability to make war.

Fighting the British Again at Sea

In the late spring of 1807, the matter grew serious in the waters of Chesapeake Bay. A pair of French battleships had docked at Annapolis for repairs. Two British ships lay at the capes of the Chesapeake, preventing the ships from reaching the open sea. In the meantime, on June 22, Commodore James Barron ordered his ship, the USS *Chesapeake*, out of its anchorage at Norfolk, Virginia, at the mouth of the Chesapeake.

Their spies in Annapolis had told the British that the *Chesapeake* was carrying several deserters, who had enlisted in the U.S. Navy. Ten miles out at sea, the HMS (His Majesty's Ship) *Leopard* drew up to the *Chesapeake*. The British captain shouted across the water, demanding to board the *Chesapeake* and take any deserters captive. Commodore Barron abruptly refused and ordered his crew to prepare for a fight. The guns aboard the *Leopard* roared to life, pouring three broadsides of shot and shell into the American ship.

The salvo tore at the planking and rigging of the *Chesapeake*. The ship drifted helplessly, unable to trim its sails and maneuver. The officers of the *Leopard* climbed aboard. They walked the decks, inspected the guns, and mustered the crew of the *Chesapeake* to the top deck. Under threat of further action by their ship, the officers took a British-born deserter and three Americans to the *Leopard*. These four men began their term of service in the king's navy immediately.

The firing on the *Chesapeake* sparked outrage in the halls of the U.S. Congress. Acting as the world's master, the British had ignored the American claim to neutrality in the king's fight with Napoléon. Some called for a declaration of war.

President Thomas Jefferson saw one possible solution in halting all commercial shipping between the United States and Europe. According to Roger Butterfield,

His policy, which he called "peaceable coercion," was a kind of controlled isolationism. At his request, Congress had already passed a law barring some British goods from entering the United States. Now a more drastic measure, the celebrated Embargo, was imposed. This prohibited all exports from all American ports. Jefferson's theory was that American food and raw materials were so necessary to the warring countries that they would soon come to terms. [32]

This action divided the Republicans but united the Federalists, who stood in fierce opposition to it. It was also strongly opposed by Maryland merchants and manufacturers who depended on foreign trade for their livelihoods. Nevertheless, the U.S. Congress passed the Embargo Act in 1807. This law made all commercial traffic between the United States and Europe illegal.

The law did not impress the British or the French. Its greatest effect was to damage American exporters, particularly the small iron and manufacturing industries of Maryland. In 1808 the entire state of Maryland exported only $2.7 million worth of goods, only about 15 percent of the previous year's amount. The Embargo Act aroused a storm of protest, and President Jefferson decided to sign a bill repealing it in 1809.

Another War Comes to Maryland

Independence had not ended the grievances of the Americans against Great Britain. The British restrictions on American trade, and the British navy's impressment (forced service) of sailors captured from U.S. ships, sparked an outright declaration of war by the U.S. government in 1812.

The people of Maryland were evenly split on the war. Many argued that the issue of impressment was not worth another fight with Great Britain, which still had the world's most powerful army and navy. Marylanders, in particular, knew their state would become a tempting target for the British, because its many waterways would allow an easy invasion by British troops and because the state lay directly on the path to the national capital of Washington, D.C.

The fighting began in June 1812, and soon the American privateers went back to work. Maryland's busiest shipyard at Fells Point turned out hundreds of fast, light clipper ships useful for overcoming slower

British ships sailed through Maryland's waterways en route to the new American capital at Washington, D.C., during the War of 1812.

British ships and running past the blockade set up by the British to stop shipments to and from Europe. In all, the Baltimore clippers captured or sank about seventeen hundred British military and merchant ships, many of them in Chesapeake Bay. The most famous privateer of them all was Captain Thomas Boyle, who sailed the *Chasseur* (French for *Hunter*) out of the Fells Point shipyard. Boyle's most famous exploit took place in 1814, when, as one historian recounts,

> Boyle unexpectedly sailed east, directly to the British Isles, where he unmercifully harassed the British merchant fleet. In a characteristically audacious act, he sent a notice to the King by way of a captured merchant vessel that he had released for the purpose. . . . In it he declared that the entire British Isles were under naval blockade by *Chasseur* alone! This affront sent the shipping community into panic and caused the Admiralty to call vessels home from the American war to guard merchant ships which had to sail in convoys.[33]

Thomas Kennedy's Beliefs

Maryland may have practiced religious tolerance, but there were limits. When it came to public office, religious belief was a requirement for all. By the Maryland constitution of 1776, only Christians were entitled to protection of their religious beliefs. In addition, the constitution required only one test for those who held public office: They must be Christians.

These articles were first challenged by Thomas Kennedy of Hagerstown, a member of Maryland's House of Delegates. In 1819 he introduced a bill to grant the same rights to Maryland's Jews and anyone else who believed in a "future state of rewards and punishments." The bill was voted down in 1819 and again in 1820. Kennedy lost his seat in 1823, but after being reelected in 1825, he reintroduced the bill, which passed. The requirement that anyone holding office in Maryland must believe in a "future state of rewards and punishments" was deleted from the Maryland constitution of 1867.

Privateers could harm the enemy but could do little to protect the people of Maryland from British forces. In early February 1813, Admiral George Cockburn and the feared British navy invaded Chesapeake Bay. The British blockaded the entire bay as well as Baltimore harbor. Troops landed at Elk River, setting off to plunder city homes and plantations on both sides of the Chesapeake. Later Cockburn conquered Kent Island, which was used as a staging area for the raids up and down the bay.

In 1814 a victory over Napoléon in Europe freed up thousands of British troops for service in North America. In August 1814 Cockburn and General Robert Ross sailed up the Patuxent River, disembarked several thousand British troops at the town of Benedict, and advanced along the dusty roads toward Washington. On August 24, at the Maryland town of Bladensburg, the British scattered an outnumbered American force led by General William Winder. The British proceeded to Washington, where they started a fire that could be seen as far away as Baltimore. While panicked citizens scrambled to safety through the streets of the capital, the White House, the Senate house, barracks, arsenals, storehouses, and private homes were put to the torch.

The British then turned on Baltimore, but they took two weeks to get underway. In the meantime, the city prepared its defenses under the leadership of General Sam Smith, the commander of the Third Division of Maryland militia. Historian Carl Bode writes,

> [Smith] took over like a cyclone. He swept together the remnants of the Maryland militia left after Bladensburg. He ordered the citizens out, with their shovels, picks, and wheelbarrows, to start digging on Hampstead Hill to fortify the eastern approaches to the city, where the British were expected. . . . He wangled a $100,000 bank loan to buy supplies, for even ammunition was lacking. As the earthworks went up so did the number of soldiers to man them. In a week's time Sam Smith had assembled under him six other generals and their commands. He directed them with the precision of a military bandmaster.[34]

On the morning of September 12, the British marched on Baltimore. General Ross was killed by a sniper, but the British regrouped. On the next day they were stopped by Smith's militia and daunting earthworks at Hampstead Hill. Meeting that night, a council of British officers voted to retreat.

At the same time, Cockburn's fleet of sixteen ships were sailing up the Patapsco River to begin a bombardment of Fort McHenry, at the entrance of Baltimore's harbor. At dawn on September 14 a Maryland lawyer watched the bombardment from a boat sailing nearby under a flag of truce. Thrilled by the sight of a defiant American flag, still flying through a thick haze of smoke from more than two thousand rockets and bombs, Francis Scott Key wrote

Francis Scott Key, composer of the "Star Spangled Banner."

down several stanzas of poetry, which would later be set to a British drinking song, "To Anacreon in Heaven" and renamed. The thick walls of Fort McHenry had stopped the British and inspired "The Star-Spangled Banner." As historian Samuel Eliot Morison writes: "Maryland militia showed a very different spirit from that of their Virginia countrymen. Naval bombardment of Fort McHenry accomplished nothing for the British, but gave us a stirring national anthem."[35]

The valiant stand of Fort McHenry convinced the British commander to turn back from Baltimore. In the town of Ghent, on the European continent, British diplomats decided to make peace with the Americans. The negotiations resulted in the Treaty of Ghent, which formally ended the war on Christmas Eve 1814. The war had depressed Maryland trade and industry, causing several companies and banks to fail. It had also practically ended the Federalist Party, which suffered a resounding defeat in the elections of 1812.

But the state would quickly recover. In 1811 a highway to the west had been inaugurated at the town of Cumberland. This National Road, which followed the valley of the Ohio River and then set off directly west through Ohio and Indiana, would become the Main Street of the trans-Appalachian west, the superhighway of settlement in the prairies between the mountains and the Mississippi River. The National Road and other busy highways guaranteed that Maryland would prosper and play a leading role in the decades of westward expansion to come.

On July 4, 1828, the people of Baltimore celebrated their victory of 1814 in a long parade in which General Sam Smith took the place of honor. The city's labor guilds celebrated their crafts with a series of fanciful parade floats built by the tailors, painters, carpenters, hatters, coachmakers, and metalworkers. Capping off the parade was the laying of the first stone of the Baltimore and Ohio (B&O) Railroad by Charles Carroll, the last surviving signer of the Declaration of Independence. In the same year, work on the Chesapeake and Ohio Canal, which would run from the Potomac River at Washington to Cumberland, Maryland, would begin. The B&O, as well as the new canals and highways, would transform the city of Baltimore and the state of Maryland into a cornerstone of American industry for decades.

Notes

Chapter One: The English Arrive in Chesapeake Bay

1. Quoted in Paul Wilstach, *Tidewater Maryland*. New York: Tudor, 1931, p. 30.
2. Matthew Page Andrews, *History of Maryland: Province and State.* Hatboro, PA: Tradition, 1965, p. 10.
3. Wilstach, *Tidewater Maryland*, p. 40.
4. Andrews, *History of Maryland*, p. 32.
5. Quoted in Andrews, *History of Maryland*, p. 216.
6. Aubrey C. Land, *Colonial Maryland. A History*. Millwood, KY: KTO, 1981, p. 35.

Chapter Two: Religious Strife in Maryland

7. "Two Acts of Toleration," April 21, 1649, Maryland State Archives, www.mdarchives.state.md.us/msa/speccol/sc2200/sc2221/000025/html/intro.html.
8. Samuel Eliot Morison, *The Oxford History of the American People.* New York: Oxford University Press, 1965, p. 85.
9. J. A. Doyle, *English Colonies in America: Virginia, Maryland, and the Carolinas.* New York: Henry Holt, 1889, p. 317.
10. Doyle, *English Colonies in America*, p. 320.
11. Doyle, *English Colonies in America*, p. 327.

Chapter Three: Daily Life in Colonial Maryland

12. Quoted in Anne Elizabeth Yentsch, *A Chesapeake Family and Their Slaves: A Study in Historical Archaeology.* New York: Cambridge University Press, 1994, p. 10.
13. Andrews, *History of Maryland*, p. 216.
14. Yentsch, *A Chesapeake Family and Their Slaves*, p. 10.
15. Charles Albro Barker, *The Background of the Revolution in Maryland.* New Haven, CT: Yale University Press, 1940, p. 69.
16. Quoted in Frederick Gutheim, *The Potomac.* New York: Rinehart, 1949, p. 72.
17. Quoted in Thad W. Tate and David L. Ammerman, *The Chesapeake in the Seventeenth Century: Essays on Anglo-American*

Society. Chapel Hill: University of North Carolina Press, 1979, p. 131.

18. Quoted in Tate and Ammerman, *The Chesapeake in the Seventeenth Century,* p. 51.

19. Land, *Colonial Maryland,* p. 103.

20. Lois Green Carr, Philip D. Morgan, and Jean B. Russo, *Colonial Chesapeake Society.* Chapel Hill: University of North Carolina Press, 1988, p. 7.

21. Andrews, *History of Maryland,* p. 216.

Chapter Four: The Revolution in Maryland

22. William Hand Browne, *Maryland: The History of a Palatinate.* Boston: Houghton Mifflin, 1904, p. 218.

23. Morison, *The Oxford History of the American People,* p. 186.

24. Browne, *Maryland,* p. 243.

25. Merrill Jensen, *The Founding of a Nation: A History of the American Revolution, 1763–1776.* New York: Oxford University Press, 1968, p. 381.

26. Jensen, *The Founding of a Nation,* p. 382.

27. Jensen, *The Founding of a Nation,* p. 693.

28. J. R. Pole, *Foundations of American Independence, 1763–1815.* Indianapolis: Bobs-Merrill, 1972, p. 141.

29. Quoted in Hubert Footner, *Rivers of the Eastern Shore: Seventeen Maryland Rivers.* New York: Farrar and Rinehart, 1944, p. 57.

Chapter Five: Federalists and Republicans in Maryland

30. Roger Butterfield, *The American Past.* New York: Simon and Schuster, 1947, p. 20.

31. Carl Bode, *Maryland: A Bicentennial History.* New York: W. W. Norton, 1978, p. 51.

32. Butterfield, *The American Past,* p. 48.

33. Quoted in "Chausseur," Pride of Baltimore II website, http://intandem.com/NewPrideSite/Other/OtherPrivate.html.

34. Bode, *Maryland,* pp. 58–59.

35. Morison, *The Oxford History of the American People,* p. 393.

Chronology

1524
Giovanni da Verrazano sails along the North American coast, passing the mouth of Chesapeake Bay.

1608
John Smith of Virginia explores Chesapeake Bay, staking a claim to the region for England.

1631
Virginia trader William Claiborne settles on Kent Island.

1632
King Charles I grants a charter to Cecilius Calvert, Lord Baltimore, for all unexplored lands north of the Potomac River as far as the southern boundary of Pennsylvania.

1634
Settlers assembled by Lord Baltimore arrive at St. Clements Island in the *Ark* and the *Dove*.

1649
The Maryland Assembly passes the Act Concerning Religion, decreeing tolerance of all Christian sects within Maryland.

1664
Slavery laws pass the Maryland Assembly; all Africans transported to or sold in Maryland must remain slaves for life.

1683
The head-right system ends in Maryland; settlers are no longer entitled to land based on the number of individuals in their household.

1692
Maryland becomes a Crown colony, to be ruled directly by the English king; in the same year, the Church of England becomes the colony's official church.

1715
The Crown restores proprietary rule in Maryland.

1729
The city of Baltimore is founded.

1732
Maryland's eastern boundary with Delaware, which comprises three southernmost counties of the Pennsylvania colony, is fixed.

1763
The survey of the Maryland-Pennsylvania border by Charles Mason and Jeremiah Dixon commences.

1765
The British Parliament approves the Stamp Act, inciting open defiance in Maryland.

1774
On October 19 the British merchant ship *Peggy Stewart* is burned in Annapolis harbor.

1776
Robert Eden, British governor of Maryland, leaves the colony on June 26; on July 4 four Maryland delegates sign the Declaration of Independence; On July 6 an assembly of Marylanders declares independence; on November 3 Maryland adopts the Declaration of Rights; on November 8 the first state constitution is adopted; on December 20 the Continental Congress convenes in Baltimore and will meet until March 4, 1777.

1781
On February 2 Loyalist land and property in Maryland is confiscated; on March 1 Maryland ratifies the Articles of Confederation.

1783
On November 26 the Continental Congress convenes at Annapolis (and will meet there until June 3, 1784); on December 23, at the State House in Annapolis, George Washington resigns his commission as commander of the Continental Army.

1784
The Continental Congress ratifies the Treaty of Paris at Annapolis.

For Further Reading

Catherine Drinker Bowen, *Miracle at Philadelphia: The Story of the Constitutional Convention, May to September 1787*. Boston: Little, Brown, 1986. A readable account of the Constitutional Convention in Philadelphia and detailed descriptions of the actions and motives of the convention's delegates.

Edwin Danson, *Drawing the Line: How Mason and Dixon Surveyed the Most Famous Border in America*. New York: John Wiley and Sons, 2000. A popular history of the drawing of the Mason-Dixon Line, explaining eighteenth-century methods of surveying and describing the tough challenges that made the Mason-Dixon survey a great scientific achievement.

Ronald Hoffman and Sally D. Mason, *Princes of Ireland, Planters of Maryland: A Carroll Saga, 1500–1782*. Raleigh: University of North Carolina Press, 2000. A chronicle of the Carroll family, Irish Catholics who settled in Maryland and who faced systematic discrimination in largely Protestant colonial America.

Deborah Kent, *Maryland*. Chicago: Childrens Press, 1990. This book gives a readable account of Maryland's geography, history, economy, and society.

Jean B. Lee, *The Price of Nationhood: The American Revolution in Charles County*. New York: W. W. Norton, 1994. A description of the society of Charles County, Maryland, located on the western shore of the Chesapeake, and how the Revolutionary movement affected members of the different classes, from landowner to slave.

Walter Lord, *The Dawn's Early Light*. Baltimore: Johns Hopkins University Press, 1994. An absorbing and action-packed account of the people and events of the War of 1812, and the crucial battles waged in and around Baltimore.

M. Christopher New, *Maryland Loyalists in the American Revolution*. Centreville, MD: Tidewater, 1996. Based on previously unpublished documents, this book traces the history of a four hundred–strong Loyalist regiment raised on the eastern shore and their hardships during the American Revolution.

Leslie Rauth, *Maryland*. New York: Marshall Cavendish, 2000. A school/library volume providing information on Maryland's geography, history, and economy, along with interesting facts about the state.

Donald G. Shomette, *Lost Towns of Tidewater Maryland*. Centreville, MD: Tidewater, 2000. An investigation into ten abandoned towns in the Tidewater region, how they came into existence, and why they disappeared.

Works Consulted

Books

Matthew Page Andrews, *History of Maryland: Province and State.* Hatboro, PA: Tradition, 1965. A facsimile edition of a classic 1929 history book, detailed and richly illustrated with source quotes by a well-known Maryland historian.

Charles Albro Barker, *The Background of the Revolution in Maryland.* New Haven, CT: Yale University Press, 1940. A history of Maryland's role in the American Revolution, focusing on the contest between proprietary government and the growing movement for liberty and independence from the mother country.

Francis F. Beirne, *The Amiable Baltimoreans.* Hatboro, PA: Tradition, 1968. An anecdotal social history of Baltimore, concerning events major and minor in the city's long history.

Carl Bode, *Maryland: A Bicentennial History.* New York: W. W. Norton, 1978. A light and brief overview of Maryland history.

William Hand Browne, *Maryland: The History of a Palatinate.* Boston: Houghton Mifflin, 1904. A history of Maryland as described through its leading personalities and politicians, focusing on the pre-Revolutionary period but continuing through the 1860s.

Robert J. Brugger, Cynthia Horsburgh Requardt, Robert I. Cottom Jr., *Maryland: A Middle Temperament, 1634–1980.* Baltimore: Johns Hopkins University Press, 1996. A general overview of Maryland history from the founding of the colony to the 1980s.

Roger Butterfield, *The American Past.* New York: Simon and Schuster, 1947. A visual history of the United States, using vintage cartoons, photographs, and illustrations from the eighteenth century to the mid–twentieth century. An excellent introduction to topics such as slavery, industialization, and other essential events and concepts in the country's history.

Lois Green Carr, Philip D. Morgan, and Jean B. Russo, *Colonial Chesapeake Society.* Chapel Hill: University of North Carolina Press, 1988. This book offers detailed, data-rich analyses by Maryland historians on the society and economy of colonial Maryland.

J. A. Doyle, *English Colonies in America: Virginia, Maryland, and the Carolinas.* New York: Henry Holt, 1889. Society and government in the southern colonies, emphasizing the effect of political rivalries in the home country, sometimes bitter infighting between governors and colonists, and different religious and political factions.

Hubert Footner, *Rivers of the Eastern Shore: Seventeen Maryland Rivers.* New York: Farrar and Rinehart, 1944. A travelogue through the towns, countryside, and wild spaces of the eastern shore.

Frederick Gutheim, *The Potomac.* New York: Rinehart, 1949. A social history of the Potomac River, from the first European explorations to the twentieth century.

Joseph Moss Ives, *The "Ark" and the "Dove": The Beginnings of Civil and Religious Liberties in America.* New York: Longmans, Green, 1936. An account of the voyage of the first of Lord Baltimore's settlers to St. Marys City, and the political and religious institutions they founded that had a lasting effect on the Maryland colony.

Merrill Jensen, *The Founding of a Nation: A History of the American Revolution, 1763–1776.* New York: Oxford University Press, 1968. Long and detailed chronicle of the Revolution, useful for readers interested in colonial political factions and in the Revolutionary events and leading characters of the individual colonies.

Mary Johnston, *Pioneers of the Old South: A Chronicle of English Colonial Beginnings.* New Haven, CT: Yale University Press, 1918. An outdated but absorbing old account of the founding of Maryland, Virginia, the Carolinas, and Georgia.

Aubrey C. Land, *Colonial Maryland: A History.* Millwood, NY: KTO, 1981. This book is part of a bicentennial history project and is a useful survey of Maryland history, emphasizing social tensions and political debates within the colony.

Samuel Eliot Morison. *The Oxford History of the American People.* New York: Oxford University Press, 1965. A comprehensive and useful reference text on American history, from the earliest Native American settlements to the death of President John F. Kennedy.

John A. Munroe, *Colonial Delaware: A History.* Millwood, NY: KTO, 1978. History of the Delaware colony, including a detailed account of the border disputes among the proprietors and governors of Maryland and Pennsylvania that brought the colony into existence.

J. R. Pole, *Foundations of American Independence, 1763–1815.* Indianapolis: Bobbs-Merrill, 1972. The Revolution and its aftermath in the early state legislatures, when the country's new institutions were being shaped by the events and leaders of the two principal factions of Federalists and Republicans.

Works Consulted

J. Thomas Scharf, *History of Maryland from the Earliest Period to the Present Day*. Hatboro, PA: Tradition, 1967. A rare, three-volume work on Maryland history, including many details on the events and personalities of the colonial period not found in modern works.

Jeffrey St. John, *Forge of Union/Anvil of Liberty: A Correspondent's Report on the First Federal Elections, the First Federal Congress, and the Bill of Rights*. Ottawa, IL: Jameson Books, 1992. This book, written as a newspaper reporter's on-the-scene account of the first federal elections, the first U.S. Congress, and the debates and intrigues that brought about the Bill of Rights.

Thad W. Tate and David L. Ammerman, *The Chesapeake in the Seventeenth Century: Essays on Anglo-American Society*. Chapel Hill: University of North Carolina Press, 1979. This book contains nine essays on daily life in colonial Maryland and Virginia, covering immigration, family life, environment, settlement patterns, politics, and social classes.

Edward Loring Tottle, *War in the Woods: The Day the United States Began, July 9, 1755*. Windham, ME: Educational Materials, 1991. A long and very detailed scholarly book on the French and Indian Wars.

T. Stephen Whitman, *The Price of Freedom: Slavery and Manumission in Baltimore and Early National Maryland*. Lexington: University Press of Kentucky, 1997. A description of the economics of slavery in Baltimore after the American Revolution and the workings of "term slavery," in which slaves and masters entered into agreements for a limited term of service to be followed by the slaves' emancipation.

Paul Wilstach, *Tidewater Maryland*. New York: Tudor, 1931. This book covers the discovery, settlement, and growth of the tidewater region, concentrating on surprising, little-known aspects of daily life.

Anne Elizabeth Yentsch, *A Chesapeake Family and Their Slaves: A Study in Historical Archaeology*. New York: Cambridge University Press, 1994. This book discusses the archaeological discoveries on a Maryland plantation site, discussing artifacts, garden plots, food, hunting, fishing, and the attributes of slavery and servitude.

Internet Sources

"Chausseur," Pride of Baltimore II website, http://intandem.com/New PrideSite/Other/OtherPrivate.html

"Two Acts of Toleration," April 21, 1649, Maryland State Archives, www.mdarchives.state.md.us/msa/speccol/sc2200/sc2221/000025/ht ml/intro.html

Index

Picture Credits

Cover: The Founding of Maryland by Tompkins Harrison,1853.
  Courtesy of the Maryland State Archives

Archive Photos:15, 71

Bettman/CORBIS: 56, 60, 63, 64, 74, 77

CORBIS: 67

Hulton Getty/Archive Photos: 41, 49

North Wind Picture Archives: 8, 19, 20, 25, 28, 43, 51

Stock Montage: 18, 21, 33, 35, 39, 46, 58, 65, 79

About the Author

Tom Streissguth has written more than 30 books of non-fiction for young readers, from *Life Among the Vikings* to *Utopian Visionaries; Lewis and Clark; Wounded Knee: The End of the Plains Indian Wars;* and the award-winning *Hustlers and Hoaxers.* He has written or collaborated on dozens of geography books as well as biographies and descriptive histories. His interests include music, languages, and travel. He has also co-founded a private language school, "Learn French!", which hosts summer tours each year in Europe. He lives in Florida with his wife and two daughters.